HOMOPHONES

Words that Sound Alike or One Reason English is Difficult to Learn

HOMOPHONES

Words that Sound Alike or One Reason English is Difficult to Learn

CHARLOTTE SMITH

SUNSTONE
PRESS

SANTA FE

Sunstone books may be purchased for educational, business, or sales promotional use.
For information please write: Special Markets Department, Sunstone Press,
P.O. Box 2321, Santa Fe, New Mexico 87504-2321.

Book and cover design › R. Ahl
Printed on acid-free paper
⊗
eBook 978-1-61139-621-8

Library of Congress Cataloging-in-Publication Data

Names: Smith, Charlotte, 1951- author.
Title: Homophones : words that sound alike or one reason English is
    difficult to learn / by Charlotte Smith.
Description: Santa Fe, NM : Sunstone Press, [2020] | Includes
    bibliographical references. | Summary: "A lighthearted guide to
    homophones for English Second Language learners or anyone who wants to
    improve their language skills"-- Provided by publisher.
Identifiers: LCCN 2021002105 | ISBN 9781632933249 (paperback) | ISBN
    9781611396218 (epub) | ISBN 1632933241 (paperback)
Subjects: LCSH: English language--Homonyms--Dictionaries.
Classification: LCC PE1595 .S65 2020 | DDC 423.1--dc23
LC record available at https://lccn.loc.gov/2021002105

WWW.SUNSTONEPRESS.COM
SUNSTONE PRESS / POST OFFICE BOX 2321 / SANTA FE, NM 87504-2321 /USA
(505) 988-4418 / FAX (505) 988-1025

Dedicated to my grandsons Levi and August

INTRODUCTION

Homonyms are a large group of multiple-meaning words. They have the same sound and often the same spelling but different meanings. The term "homonym" comes from the Greek words "homos" (same) and "onuma" (name). This large group of homonyms includes words like lie (not tell the truth) and lie (recline or rest) and also words like see (use your eyes) and sea (the ocean).

A homophone is a type of homonym. Homophones sound alike but have different meanings and different spellings, like see and sea. The term "homophone" comes from the Greek words "homos" (same) and "phone" (sound). There are hundreds of homophones. This book lists those that may help English as a second language learners (ESL) the most in their study of the English language. Furthermore, this book will benefit anyone who wants to improve his or her English. Some words are not pronounced exactly the same way but are very similar.

Homographs are words with the same spelling, but they may or may not sound the same. For example, lie (recline) and lie (not tell the truth) are in this group. Wind (air blowing, short i sound) and wind (to twist something, long i sound) are also in this group. The term "homograph" comes from the Greek words "homos" (same) and "graphe" (writing).

Finally, there is a special type of homograph called a heteronym. Heteronyms are words that have the same spelling but different sounds, like wind (air) and wind (twist), tear (moisture in the eye) and tear (to rip), present (accent on the first syllable) and present (accent on the second syllable), record (accent on the first syllable) and record (accent on the second syllable) to name a few.

These are the eight parts of English speech:

noun (n.): persons, places, or things
pronoun (pron.): takes the place of a noun, for example, I, you, me,
he, they, it
verb (v.): shows action or a state of being
adjective (adj.): modifies a noun or pronoun
adverb (adv.): modifies a verb, adjective, or other adverb
preposition (prep.): words that show position
conjunction (conj.): connecting words
interjection (inter.): a type of exclamation

A

able: adj.; skillful, capable
Abel: n.; second son of Adam, who slew his brother Cain

acclamation: n.; praise
acclimation: n.; becoming accustomed to a new climate or condition

acknowledgment: n.; acceptance of the truth of something; statement of indebtedness to others, especially at the beginning or end of a book
acknowledgement: n.; British spelling of acknowledgment

acts: n.; plural of act (deed; things done; a pretense or false display)
     v.; part of the verb to act (behave; take action; do something)
ax (or axe): n.; sharp tool for chopping; slang for guitar
      v.; to end suddenly

ad: n.; advertisement
add: v.; to increase or join or total numbers to find a sum

ade: n.; drink based on fruit juice
aid: n.; help
   v.; to help
aide: n.; a helper

adherence: n.; attachment
adherents: n.; supporters

ado: n.; trouble or fuss
adieu: inter.; goodbye
     n.; a goodbye

ads: n.; advertisements
adds: v.; totals numbers to find a sum
adze (or adz): n.; sharp tool like an ax

adolescents: n.; teenagers
adolescence: n.; the state of being a teenager

aegis: n.; the protection and support of a person or organization
egis: n.; alternate spelling of aegis

aerial: n.; an antenna
      adj.; of the air
Ariel: n.; character in a Shakespeare play

ail: v.; to be sick
ale: n.; a type of beer

air: n.; wind or breeze
e'er: adv.; poetic for ever
ere: adv.; poetic for before
err: v.; to make a mistake
heir: n.; one who inherits something

aired: v.; ventilated
erred: v.; past tense of to err (make a mistake)

airy: adj.; windy or breezy
aerie: n.; an eagle's nest

aisle: n.; walkway
isle: n.; small island
I'll: contraction for I will

ait: n.; small island
ate: v.; past tense of eat (put food into the mouth, chew, and swallow)
eight: n.; the number 8

align: v.; to bring into line
aline: v.; British spelling of align

all: n.; the whole amount
awl: n.; tool for making holes

allowed: v.; past tense of allow (to give permission to do something)
aloud: adv.; not silent

allusive: adj.; referring to something else
elusive: adj.; hard to find or catch
illusive: adj.; not what it seems or deceptive

already: adv.; before
all ready: adj.; completely prepared

alter: v.; to change
altar: n.; place to worship

altogether: adv.; totally or completely
all together: in a group

always: adv.; forever
all ways: in every single way

ameba: n.; a one-celled animal
amoeba: alternate spelling of ameba

an: adj.; a, but used before a word starting with a vowel (a, e, i, o, or u)
Ann (or Anne): n.; a girl's name

analog: adj.; relating to or using signals or information represented by a continuous variable
     n.; a person or thing seen as comparable to another
analogue: British spelling of analog

analyst: n.; one who studies or analyzes
annalist: n.; a recorder or historian

annalize: v.; to record or write annals of
analyze: v.; to study or question or investigate
analyse: v.; British spelling of analyze

ant: n.; an insect
aunt: n.; the sister of one's father or mother

ante: n.; a stake in poker
anti: prep; against
    adj.; opposed
    n.; one opposed to something
auntie: n.; uncle's wife
aunty: n.; alternate spelling of auntie

antecedence: n.; act of going before
antecedents: n.; ancestors of your family

apologize: v.; to say you're sorry for something you did wrong
apologise: v.; British spelling of apologize

apps: n.; plural of app (an application downloaded by a computer user to a mobile device)
apse: n.; a recess in a church, usually containing the altar

arc: n.; part of a circle
ark: n.; a boat or a holy box

ardor: n.; passion or enthusiasm or excitement
ardour: n.; British spelling of ardor

Aries: n.; first astrological sign in the zodiac, the Ram
Ares: n.; Greek god of war
aeries: n.; plural of aerie (a large nest of a bird of prey, especially an eagle)

armor: n.; a metal covering of the body for protection
armour: n.; British spelling of armor

arrant: adj.; bad or wicked
errant: adj.; wandering or roving

ascent: n.; act of going up
assent: n.; agreement or consent

assistants: n.; helpers
assistance: n.; help or aid

ate: v.; past tense of eat
eight: n.; the number 8
ait: n.; small island

attendance: n.; act of being there
attendants: n.; those who attend or serve

auger: n.; tool for making holes in wood
augur: v.; to predict or foretell
        n.; a religious official in ancient Rome who observed natural signs and interpreted them as indication of approval or disapproval of an action; one who foretells events by omens

aught: n.; zero or 0
ought: v.; must or should

aural: adj.; having to do with hearing
oral: adj.; spoken

auricle: n.; outer ear
oracle: n.; a seer or prophet or fortune teller

authorize: v.; give permission for some act
authorise: v.; British spelling of authorize

away: adv.; at a distance
aweigh: adj.; of an anchor raised to clear the bottom of the sea

awful: adj.; can mean bad or inspiring awe
offal: n.; trash or rubbish or sewage

ax: n.; tool used for chopping wood; slang for a musical instrument
    v.; to end suddenly
axe: British spelling of ax

axel: n.; a skating jump
axle: n.; bar on which wheels rotate

axis: n.; turning line or pivot
axes: n.; plural of ax or plural of axis

aye: inter.; yes
ay: inter.; alternate spelling of aye
eye: n.; organ of sight
I: pron.; myself

B

B: n.: the second letter of the English alphabet
be: v.; to exist
bee: n.; an insect; the letter B
Bea: n.; a female name, short for Beatrice

baa: inter.; cry of sheep
bah: inter.; exclamation of disagreement

bad: adj.; evil or wicked
bade: v.; past tense of bid (offer a certain price for something; utter a greeting or farewell to; order someone to do something; invite someone to do something)

bade: v.; alternate pronunciation of bade above, with a long a instead of short a
bayed: v.; barked or yelped, past tense of bay

bail: n.; temporary release of one accused of a crime; several other meanings in the fields of technology, climbing, fishing, and sports
     v.; to let a prisoner out of jail after paying bail; to take a bucket and scoop water out of a boat; to abandon a responsibility
bale: n.; a parcel or bundle
bell: n.; a metal object that sounds a musical note when tapped
belle: n.; a beautiful woman, especially the most beautiful one in a group
bel: n.; a measure of sound

bailer: n.; one who bails (scoops water out of a boat; abandons a commitment or obligation)
baler: n.; one who bundles

bait: n.; a lure or decoy
    v.; to lure or tempt
bate: v.; to lessen or decrease

bald: adj.; without hair
balled: v.; formed into a ball (spherical object)
bawled: v.; cried

balks: v.; part of the verb to balk (hesitate or not want to accept an idea)
box: n.; container, usually a square or rectangle in shape

ball: n.; a round sphere; a dance or party
bawl: v.; to cry or weep

balm: n.; lotion or ointment
bomb: n.; explosive

band: n.; a group of musicians
banned: v.; past tense of the verb to ban (not allow)
    adj.; not allowed

bands: n.; groups of musicians
bans: v.; part of the verb to ban (prohibit or not allow to happen)
banns: n.; announcements in church for upcoming marriage

bar: n.; a long rod; a counter where alcohol is served
    v.; fasten something with a bar, especially a door or window; to keep
someone from doing something
barre: n.; the horizontal bar that ballet dancers use

bard: n.; poet
barred: v.; past tense of verb to bar (stop or prevent)
    adj.; having bars

bare: adj.; unclothed or naked
bear: n.; an animal
    v.; to endure

baring: v.; stripping or uncovering
bearing: n.; the position of something; a way of standing or behavior
Bering: n.; a strait or a sea between Alaska and Siberia

bark: n.; sharp cry of an animal, for example, a dog; outer protection of trees; thin sheets of chocolate; old-fashioned word for a ship
     v.; to make a barking sound; to call out to sell something
barque: n.; British spelling of bark, a ship

baron: n.; a nobleman
barren: adj.; childless or sterile; unproductive land

baroness: n.; a noblewoman
barrenness: n.; the state of being barren (see above)

base: n.; foundation or support
     adj.; mean or vile
     v.; use as a point of development
bass: n.; the lowest male singing voice

based: v.; past tense of base (see above)
     adj.; having a specified basis
baste: v.; to sew loosely; moisten, as in cooking a turkey

bases: n.; plural of base (see above)
basis: n.; underlying foundation for an idea or process or a stand or support

bask: v.; to lie in the sun
Basque: n.; a race of people in France or Spain

bay: n.; an inlet of the ocean where the land curves inward; a recess in a mountain range; a type of shrub; a type of window; a type of compartment; the sound of dogs baying (howling loudly)
     v.; of a dog, to bark loudly
     adj.; of a horse, brown and black
bey: n.; formerly used in Turkey and Egypt as a title of respect; a governor in the Ottoman Empire
bae: n.; slang, short for babe or baby, as to boyfriends and girlfriends

bays: n.; plural of the noun bay (see above)
beys: n.; plural of bey (see above)
baes: n.; plural of bae (see above)
baize: n.; a type of coarse, woolen material, especially for covering pool tables

bazaar: n.; a market or a sale of goods, usually for charity
bizarre: adj.; odd or strange

beach: n.; the edge of water or seashore
beech: n.; type of tree

beat: v.; to hit or strike; in cooking, to mix; to defeat in a game
       n.; a main accent in music
beet: n.; a vegetable

Beatles: n.; a famous British band
beetles: n.; plural of beetle (a type of insect)

beau: n.; boyfriend
bow: n.; a weapon used with arrows; a hair adornment

beaut: n.; informal for a fine example of something
butte: n.; similar to a mesa but narrower

been: v.; part of the verb to be
Ben: n.; a male name, short for Benjamin
bin: n.; a container

beer: n.; ale or a type of alcohol
bier: n.; coffin or casket

behavior: n.; the way in which one acts
behaviour: n.; British spelling of behavior

bell: n.; a metal object that sounds a musical note when struck
belle: n.; a beautiful female, especially the most beautiful in a group
bail: n.; bond, for one in jail
      v.; to dip or scoop; to get someone out of jail
bale: n.; parcel or bundle
bel: n.; a measure of sound

berg: n.; big mass of ice, short for iceberg
burg: n.; a small town

berry: n.; a small fruit
bury: v.; put in a grave

berth: n.; a small bed, as on a train
birth: n.; act of being born or the start of something

better: adj.; more excellent
bettor: n.; a gambler

billed: v.; past tense of to bill (give a statement to one who owes someone else money)
      adj.; having a bill or beak
build: v.; to construct or make

bite: v.; to eat or chew
      n.; a piece of food
bight: n.; part of a rope; a creek
byte: n.; a group of binary digits in technology

blew: v.; past tense of blow (to move creating a current of air; expel air through lips)
blue: adj.; a color; sad
bleu: adj.; French for blue; a type of cheese

bloc: n.; a number of people acting as one group or assembly
block: n.; a cube of wood
      v.; to clog or stop up or plug

boar: n.; a male hog
boor: n; an unrefined, ill-mannered person
bore: v.; to make a hole; to tire someone due to dullness
          n.; hollow part inside a gun barrel or tube; someone or something who is dull and not interesting
Boer: n.; a member of the Dutch and Huguenot population that settled in southern Africa in the late 17th century
          adj.; relating to the Boers
Bohr: n.; Danish physicist

board: n.; a piece of wood or a plank
bored: adj.; the feeling of weariness due to dullness

boarder: n.; a person who stays somewhere
border: n.; the edge of something

bode: v.; to foretell
bowed: adj.; bent

bold: adj.; brave
bowled: v.; rolled balls in the sport of bowling

bolder: adj.; braver
boulder: n.; a rock

boll: n.; a ball of cotton
bowl: n.; a type of dish

boos: n.; plural of boo (a call of dislike)
booze: n.; slang for alcoholic liquor

bootie: n.; a soft shoe for a baby; a lady's short boot
booty: n.; stolen goods; something won; slang for one's buttocks or behind

born: v.; brought into life
borne: v.; carried
bourn: n.; a small stream
bourn (or bourne): n.; a boundary or a goal

borough: n.; a town
burro: n.; a donkey
burrow: v.; to make a hole or tunnel
        n.; a hole or tunnel dug by an animal

bough: n.; a limb on a tree
bow: v.; bend the upper part of the body as a sign of respect

bouillon: n.; a clear soup
bullion: n.; silver or gold

boy: n.; a male child
buoy: n.; a marker in a body of water, also pronounced "booey"

brae: n.; hillside
bray: v.; to make the sound of a burro
        n.; the sound of a donkey or burro

braid: n.; plaited hair
brayed: v.; past tense of bray (see above)

braise: v.; a cooking term meaning to stew
brays: v.; makes the sound of a donkey
braze: v.; to burn or to join together

brake: v.; to slow down
        n.; part of a vehicle that makes it slow down
break: v.; to separate into pieces
        n.; a pause in work; a crack or fracture

breach: n.; a division or break or failing to follow a law
breech: n.; part of a cannon;
      v.; to dress a boy in breeches (old-fashioned or archaic term for pants)

bread: n.; food made of flour
bred: v.; past tense of breed (when animals mate and have babies)

bream: n.; a type of fish
brim: n.; the edge around the bottom of a hat
      v.; be full to overflowing

breath: n.; air taken into the lungs
breadth: n.; width

breathalyze: v.; (of the police) use a breathalyzer to measure the amount of alcohol in one's breath
breathalyse: v.; British spelling of breathalyze

brewed: v.; past tense of brew (to make beer or coffee or tea)
brood: n.; a family
      v.; to think deeply about something

brews: n.; plural of brew (see above)
bruise: n.; an injury on the skin caused by a blow or hit
      v.; to cause to bruise

bridal: adj.; of the bride or a wedding
bridle: n.; headgear to control a horse
      v.; to put a bridle on a horse

Britain: n.; the United Kingdom
Briton: n.; a person born in Britain

broach: v.; to mention a subject or begin; to penetrate
brooch: n.; a piece of jewelry (a pin)

brows: n.; plural of brow (forehead); short for eyebrows
browse: v.; to look at something in an easy manner
       n.; the act of looking at something casually

burro: n.; a donkey
burrow: v.; to make a tunnel or hole, especially an animal; investigate
       n.; a hole dug by an animal

bus: n.; a large motor vehicle
     v.; to carry people on a bus
buss: v.; to kiss
      n.; a kiss

but: conj.; however or except
butt: n.; a push given with the head; buttocks or posterior; part of a gun; part of a cigar or cigarette; a person or thing at which unkind humor is directed
     v.; to hit someone with the head; to join

buy: v.; to purchase
      n.; a purchase
by: prep.; near
bye: inter.; short for goodbye

buyer: n.; one who makes a purchase
byre: n.; a British cowshed

C

C: n.; the third letter of the English alphabet; Roman numeral for 100
cee: n.; the letter C

cache: n.; a collection of items in a hidden place
      v.; to hide
cash: n.; money
      v.; to give money for a check or money order

caddie: n.; a golfer's helper
      v.; to work as a caddie
caddy: n.; a small storage container, usually with divisions

Cain: n.; the oldest son of Adam and Eve, who killed his brother Abel
cane: n.; a stick to aid in walking

cairn: n.; a pile of stones built as a landmark of some sort; a type of dog
Karen: n.; a female name; slang for entitled white woman

caliber: n.; the quality of someone's character or their ability; the diameter of a gun barrel
calibre: n.; a more common spelling of caliber in Britain

callous: adj.; cruel and insensitive
      n.; another spelling of callus
callus: n.; thicker, hardened part of the skin

Calvary: n.; place outside Jerusalem where Jesus was crucified
cavalry: n.; soldiers who fought on horses

can: n.; a metal container
v.; to be able to do; to preserve food in a container
Cannes: n.; city in France

canceled: v.; past tense of to cancel (decide a planned event will not take place; negate the effect of another)
cancelled: v.; preferred British spelling of canceled

candor: n.; honesty and frankness
candour: n.; British spelling of candor

cannon: n.; a large gun on wheels
canon: n.; a law or principle by which something is judged

can't: contraction for cannot
cant: n.; talk, usually religious or political

canter: n.; the gait of a horse between a trot and a gallop
v.; to move at a canter
cantor: n.; chanter

canvas: n.; a strong type of cloth usually for sails and tents
canvass: v.; to try to get votes for something

capital: n.; the most important city in a region, usually the seat of government; wealth in the form of money or assets
adj.; having to do with the death penalty
capitol: n.; a legislative building
Capitol: n.; the building in Washington, DC

carat: n.; a unit of weight for gems
caret: n.; a mark that means something is to be inserted
carrot: n.; a vegetable
karat: n.; a measure of the purity of gold

caries: n.; tooth decay
carries: v.; moves something from one place to another

carol: n.; a Christmas song
Carol: n.; a female name
Carroll: n.; a male name
carrel (or carrell): n.; a small space for studying alone

carry: v.; support and move from one place to another; travel, like a voice; assume responsibility for
        n.; the act of carrying
Carey: n.; a last name
Carrey: n.; a last name
Carrie: n.; a female name
Cary: n.; a male name

cart: n.; a wagon
        v.; to haul something
carte: n.; menu

cast: n.; an object made by shaping a material in a mold; the act of throwing something
        v.; to throw something
caste: n.; a system of dividing society into classes

catalog: n.; complete list of items
        v.; to make such a list
catalogue: British spelling of catalog

caudal: adj.; having to do with a tail
coddle: v.; to treat in an overprotective way

cause: n.; starting point or origin; a principle one defends
        v.; make something happen, usually bad
caws: n.; sounds of crows or ravens

cedar: n.; a type of tree
ceder: n.; one who gives in or yields
seeder: n.; a person or thing that plants seeds

cede: v.; to yield or surrender
seed: n.; a flowering plant's reproductive capability; a man's semen
      v.; to sow land with seed

ceiling: n.; overhead of a room
sealing: v.; closing or securing

cell: n.; a small room, usually a jail cell; in biology, the smallest unit in an organism
sell: v.; to give something for money
      n.; the act of selling
cel: n; a transparent sheet of celluloid upon which cartoons can be drawn

cellar: n.; basement
seller: n.; one who sells (see above)

cense: v.; to perfume with incense
cents: n.; plural of cent (one penny)
scents: n.; plural of scent (smell or odor)

censer: n.; a container for incense
censor: n.; an inspector who looks at books, etc., to see if they are obscene
      v.; to examine to see if acceptable

census: n.; official count of a population
senses: n.; plural of sense (one of five: sight, smell, hearing, taste, and touch; a feeling about something)
      v.; perceives with one of the senses

cent: n.; one penny
scent: n.; an odor or smell
sent: v.; past tense of send (cause to go to a certain place)

center: n.; the middle point of a circle or sphere
v.; to place in the middle
centre: n.; British spelling of center

centralize: v.; control under one authority
centralise: v.; British spelling of centralize

cereal: n.; a breakfast food
serial: n.; something published on a regular basis
adj.; having to do with a series; with respect to a criminal,
committing the same crime over and over

Ceres: n.; Roman god of agriculture and fertility; today, it is the name of an
asteroid or a city in California
series: n.; a list of things coming right after the other; a set of related
television or radio programs

cession: n.; giving up of something
session: n.; a meeting

champagne: n.; a type of wine
Champaign: n.; a city in Illinois

chance: n.; the possibility of something happening
adj.; accidental
chants: n.; plural of chant (a repeated phrase, usually by a crowd of people)

characterize: v.; describe the features of
characterise: British spelling of characterize

chased: v.; past tense of chase (to follow)
chaste: adj.; innocent or clean or virginal

cheap: adj.; not costing much money
cheep: n.; sound of a bird
v.; to make a shrill chirp

check: v.; to examine something for correctness
        n.; an examination to test quality of something
cheque: n.; British spelling of check
Czech: n.; a native of the Czech Republic

chews: v.; bites food to make it easier to swallow
choose: v.; to select someone or something as the best

chi: n.; the 22nd letter of the Greek alphabet
Kai: n.; a male name

chic: adj.; stylish or fashionable
sheik: n.; an Arab leader

chile: n.; U. S. spelling of chili
chili: n.; a small hot-tasting pod used in sauces, etc.
chilly: adj.; cold
Chile: n.; country in South America

choir: n.; a group of singers, usually religious
quire: n.; today, one-twentieth of a ream (500 sheets) of paper

choler: n.; outdated word for anger
collar: n.; a band of material around a piece of clothing
        v.; to arrest

choral: adj.; composed for or sung by a chorus or choir
coral: n.; the hard substance that forms reefs in the ocean

chorale: n.; a type of musical composition
corral: n.; a place for livestock, cattle and horses
        v.; gather together and confine; put animals in a corral

chord: n.; a group of notes played together
        v.; to play, arrange, or sing notes in chords
cord: n.; rope or twine; a fabric, like corduroy
cored: v.; past tense of to core (remove the center from a fruit)

chute: n.; a slide or tube; a narrow enclosure to restrain livestock; short for parachute
shoot: v.; to wound or kill a person or animal; to move quickly
      n.; a young branch coming from the main body of a tree or plant
      inter.; an exclamation

cite: v.; to mention or quote; to praise someone, usually in the armed forces
sight: n.; vision or eyesight
      v.; to see something; take aim using a gun
site: n.; position or area or location

civilization: n.; advanced stage of human development and organization
civilisation: n.; British spelling of civilization

clause: n.; a unit in the study of grammar; part of a sentence; part of a treaty or bill
claws: n.; nails or talons on an animal
Claus: n.; male first name or last name of Santa

clew: n.; part of a sail on a sailboat
      v.; to haul up the clews of a sail
clue: n.; piece of information used in solving a crime; an indication of what letters are to be placed in a puzzle
      v.; to tell someone about a certain matter

climb: v.; to go up or ascend
      n.; an ascent by climbing
clime: n.; climate or weather

close: v.; to shut; to end
clothes: n.; materials that you wear

coal: n.; a substance used as fuel
Cole: n.; a male name
kohl: n.; black powder used as eye makeup, especially in Eastern countries

coarse: adj.; rough
course: n.; path or direction or route

coat: n.; jacket or outer garment; a covering, as in paint
     v.; to give a covering to
cote: n.; a shelter for animals or birds

cob: n.; central part of an ear of corn
Cobb: n.; a last name

coffer: n.; a small chest to hold valuables
cougher: n.; one who coughs (expels air from the lungs suddenly)

cokes: n.; short for coca colas
coax: v.; to gently persuade someone to do something

colonel: n.; an army officer
kernel: n.; a seed in a nut

color: n.; hue or tint
     v.; to paint or dye something to change its color
colour: British spelling of color

complacence: n.; self-satisfaction; smugness
complaisance: n.; willingness to please others

complacent: adj.; showing smug satisfaction with oneself
complaisant: adj.; willing to please others

complement: n.; something that brings to perfection; something that makes a group complete
     v.; to make perfect
compliment: n.; polite praise or admiration
     v.; to praise someone or something

confidant (or confidante): n.; one with whom you share private matters
confident: adj.; self-assured; showing confidence in oneself

conquered: v.; past tense of conquer (take control by using military force); successfully overcame a problem
concord: n.; agreement; treaty; peace
Concord: n.; capital of the state of New Hampshire in the United States and also the name of cities in other states
Concorde: n.; supersonic airline produced by America and France, operating from 1969-2003

consonance: n.; agreement between opinions; consonants (letters that are not vowels) that are close to each other, in literature
consonants: n.; letters in the alphabet that are not vowels (a, e, i, o, and u)

coo: n.; the sound of pigeons and doves
coup: n.; an overthrow of power or a takeover

coop: n.; a cage for poultry (chickens)
       v.; to put in a cage
coupe: n.; a type of car

cops: n.; plural of cop (a policeman or policewoman)
       v.; catches or arrests a criminal; get something good, illegal or not; cops to means confesses to; cops a plea means to engage in plea bargaining in court
copse: n.; a small group of trees

core: n.; inner part
       v.; to remove the inner part from a fruit
corps: n.; branch of military service

correspondence: n.; communication
correspondents: n.; people who correspond (communicate with each other); plural of correspondent

councillor: n.; member of a council
counselor: n.; one who counsels someone else

counsel: v.; give advice to someone
        n.; advice; lawyer(s) on a case
council: n.; a group of people meeting formally and regularly
consul: n.; one appointed to live in a foreign place to protect the citizens

courier: n.; messenger or runner
currier: n.; one who works with leather; one who combs horses

coward: n.; one with no courage
cowered: v.; past tense of cower (to crouch down in fear)

coy: adj.; shy or modest
koi: n.; a type of colorful fish originally from Japan

cozy: adj.; giving a feeling of warmth and comfort
        n.; a soft covering to keep something hot or cold
cosy: British spelling of cozy

creak: v.; to make a harsh and high-pitched sound
        n.; a harsh scraping or squeaking sound
creek: n.; a small brook or stream

cretin: n.; stupid person
Cretan: adj.; related to the Greek island of Crete

crewel: n.; a type of yarn for embroidery
cruel: n.; mean and unkind

crews: n.; plural of crew (a group of people working on a form of transportation)
cruise: n.; a voyage on a ship or boat
        v.; to sail
cruse: n.; a bottle to hold liquids
Cruz: n.; a last name

criticize: v.; state the faults of someone or something; judge a literary or artistic work
criticise: v.; British spelling of criticize

cue: n.; a clue or hint; a stick used in playing pool
      v.; to give a cue to
queue: n.; a line of people waiting
       v.; to line up

curb: n.; edging to a street; a check or restraint on something
      v.; keep in check or restrain
kerb: n.; British spelling of curb; a type of bit used in horseback riding; a swelling on a horse's leg

currant: n.; a type of raisin
current: adj.; happening now
         n.; a body of water or air

curt: adj.; rudely brief
Kurt: n.; a male name

cutter: n.; a person or thing that cuts something; a fast, light patrol boat
Qatar: n.; country in the Middle East

cygnet: n.; a young swan
signet: n.; an official stamp or seal

cymbal: n.; a musical instrument
symbol: n.; a thing that stands for something else

cypress: n.; a type of tree
Cyprus: n.; Eastern Mediterranean island north of Turkey

D

D: n.; the fourth letter of the English alphabet; Roman numeral for 500
dee: n.; the letter D

dam: n.; a wall to stop water flow
     v.; to build a dam across a lake or river
damn: inter.; a curse word
      v.; to condemn

dammed: v.; past tense of the verb to dam (see above)
damned: v.; condemned

Dane: n.; one from Denmark
deign: v.; do something that someone considers beneath one's dignity

dawn: n.; right before sunrise; the beginning of something
      v.; to begin; to be understood
don: v.; to put on a piece of clothing
Don: n.; a male name, short for Donald; an honorific title, as in the Mafia

days: n.; plural of day (24 hours)
daze: v.; to make someone unable to think or react
      n.; the state of being confused

deal: n.; an agreement between two or more people
      v.; to hand out cards in a card game; take part in a trade
dill: n.; a type of herb

dear: n.; one who is loved
deer: n.; an animal

defense: n.; act of protecting from attack; case on behalf of one accused in a lawsuit
defence: n.; British spelling of defense

demeanor: n.; outward behavior
demeanour: n.; British spelling of demeanor

dense: adj.; thick; stupid
dents: n.; plural of dent (a small depression made by a blow or hit)
      v.; puts a dent in something

dependence: n.; the state of relying on someone; addiction to alcohol or drugs
dependents: n.; plural of dependent (one who relies on another, especially for money)

depravation: n.; the act of making bad or corrupting
deprivation: n.; lack of basic necessities

descendant: n.; something or someone that has come down from an ancestor
descendent: adj.; descending from an ancestor

descent: n.; the action of going down; the background of a person
dissent: n.; disagreement with another about an issue
      v.; to hold a different opinion

desert: v.; to run away from or to leave
dessert: n.; something sweet usually eaten at the end of a meal

deviser: n.; one who devises (plans by careful thought)
devisor: n.; one who devises property in a will (leaves real estate to one)
divisor: n.; a number by which another number is to be divided

dialed: v.; past tense of dial (to call a telephone number)
dialled: v.; British spelling of dialed

dialogue: n.; conversation
          v.; take part in a conversation
dialog: in American English, it has a specific use, as in dialog box

die: v.; to pass away or expire or stop living
          n.; singular form of dice, in gaming; a tool for cutting
dye: n.; a substance used to change the color of something
          v.; to change the color of something

died: v.; past tense of to die (see above)
dyed: v.; past tense of to dye (see above)

dine: v.; to eat
dyne: n.; in physics, a unit of force

dinghy: n.; a small boat for recreation or racing, especially an open boat with a mast and sails
dingy: adj.; not too bright or smart, as a person

dire: adj.; grim or terrible or awful
dyer: n.; one who dyes or applies color (see above)

disc: n.; a flat, thin round object
disk: n.; alternate spelling of disc

discreet: adj.; careful or cautious
discrete: adj.; separate and distinct

discussed: v.; past tense of discuss (to talk about something with someone else)
disgust: n. a feeling of strong disapproval
          v.; to cause someone to feel strong disapproval

do: v.; to perform an action
     n.; short for hairdo; a party
dew: n.; drops of water that form at night on grass, etc.
due: adj.; expected at a certain time
     n.; one's right to something; a type of fee
     adv.; as to direction, directly

do: n.; a musical note
doe: n.; a female deer
dough: n.; a mixture used for making bread; slang for money

doc: n.; slang for doctor
dock: n.; wharf or pier or place to keep boats

does: n.; plural of doe (a deer)
doughs: n.; plural of dough (mix to make bread)
doze: v.; to sleep or nap

done: v.; part of the verb to do
     adj.; food cooked thoroughly; no longer happening
dun: n.; a demand for payment; a dull grayish-brown color
     v.; to make repeated demands for the payment of a debt

dos: n.; Spanish for the number 2
dose: n.; an amount of medicine taken
     v.; to give someone a dose of medicine

dost: v.; old term that is part of the verb to do
dust: n.; tiny particles of matter lying on a surface, especially in the house
     v.; to perform the act of removing dust particles

draft: n.; an early version of a piece of writing; mandatory recruitment for military service; an order to pay a certain sum or a check; a current of cool air
     v.; to prepare an early form of a piece of writing; to choose someone for a special purpose
     adj.; beer not from a bottle or can; an animal used for pulling heavy loads
draught: British spelling of draft

drier: adj.; more dry (not wet)
dryer: n.; a machine to dry clothes or other things

dual: adj.; having two parts
duel: n.; a contest between two people with weapons
      v.; to fight a duel with someone

ducked: v.; past tense of duck (to lower the head suddenly or to dodge); avoided (an issue); left quickly; avoided a blow by moving down quickly; avoided something unpleasant; plunged one's head underwater briefly
duct: n.; a passageway in a building for liquid or air or cables

duffel: n.; sporting equipment; a coarse woolen cloth
duffle: n.; alternate spelling of duffel

dug: v.; past tense of dig (break up dirt and move it or to push something into)
Doug: n.; a male name, short for Douglas

dyeing: v.; part of the verb to dye (to color a fabric)
dying: adj.; to the point of death
      v.; part of the verb to die (to stop living)

E

earn: v.; to gain money by labor or service
erne: n.; a sea eagle
urn: n.; a type of vase

earnest: adj.; sincere or serious
Ernest: n.; a male name

eau: n.; French for water
oh: inter.; expression of surprise
owe: v.; obligation to pay, especially money, in return for something received

eave: n.; the edge of a roof
eve: n.; the night before, especially of a holiday
Eve: n.; a female name; the first woman, in the Bible

eek: inter.; an exclamation of alarm
eke: v.; to barely make a living

e'er: adv.; poetic for ever
ere: adv.; before
err: v.; to make a mistake
heir: n.; the person entitled to the property of another upon that person's death
air: n.; the invisible gas we breathe
    v.; to expose a room to air; to state an opinion in public

eerie: n.; weird or strange
Erie: n.; a city in Pennsylvania or Colorado; a canal in New York; one of the Great Lakes

eight: n.; the number 8
ate: v.; past tense of eat (put food in the mouth and chew and swallow it)
ait: n.; a small island

elicit: v.; to draw out a response from someone
illicit: adj.; forbidden by law or custom

elusion: n.; act of eluding (escaping from a danger)
illusion: n.; something interpreted incorrectly
allusion: n.; a reference to something else, usually from literature or history, for example

emerge: v.; to come into view; to become known
immerge: v.; to plunge or immerse in something

emigrant: n.; a person who leaves his or her own country to live in another
immigrant: n.; a person who comes to live in a foreign country

eminent: adj.; great or important
immanent: adj.; built-in or basic
imminent: adj.; about to happen

emir: n.; a Muslim title
amir: n.; alternate spelling of emir
ameer: n.; less common spelling of emir

emphasize: v.; lay stress on a word or phrase when speaking
emphasise: v.; British spelling of emphasize

employ: v.; give work to someone with pay; make use of
n.; state of being employed
employee: n.; one employed for salary

encyclopedia: n.; book or set of books giving information on many subjects, arranged alphabetically
encyclopaedia: n.; British spelling of encyclopedia

endeavor: v.; try hard
                n.; an attempt to achieve a goal
endeavour: British spelling of endeavor

energize: v.; give pep and enthusiasm to
energise: v.; British spelling of energize

enroll: v.; officially register as a member of an institution
enrol: v.; alternate spelling of enroll

eon: n.; a very long period of time; in astronomy and geology, it is one billion years
aeon: n.; alternate spelling of eon

eruption: n.; an issuing forth suddenly
irruption: n.; a breaking or bursting in

essay: n; a short piece of writing on a certain subject
ese: n.; in Spanish, used as a form of address for a man

esthetic: adj.; concerned with beauty
aesthetic: adj.; alternate spelling of esthetic

ewe: n.; a female sheep
yew: n.; a type of evergreen tree
you: pron.; the one you are addressing; yourself
ew: inter.; used to show disgust or distaste

ewes: n.; plural of ewe (female sheep)
use: v.; to employ something to achieve a result
yews: n.; plural of yew (a type of evergreen tree)

expedience: n.; the quality of being fit to give some desired end
expedients: n.; methods or plans or solutions or resources

expense: n.; money spent on something
expence: n.; British spelling of expense

eye: n.; organ of sight
I: pron.; me or myself
aye: inter.; yes

eyed: v.; past tense of eye (to look at)
      adj.; having eyes
I'd: contraction for I would, I had, or I should

eyelet: n.; a little hole in cloth or leather in which to thread a lace, string, etc.
      v.; to make an eyelet
islet: n.; a small island

F

fain: adv.; old-fashioned term meaning with pleasure or gladly
      adj.; pleased or willing
fane: n.; place of worship
feign: v.; to pretend or to fake

faint: adj.; hardly noticeable; dizzy
      v.; to pass out or black out
      n.; a blackout
feint: n.; a pretended hit
      v.; to make a pretend hit especially when angry

fair: adj.; keeping with rules or honest; light or blond
      adv.; without cheating
fare: n.; money to be paid for public transportation; food of a certain type
      v.; perform in a certain way in a certain situation or over a period of
time

fairy: n.; sprite or elf or imaginary being
ferry: n.; a boat to carry passengers a short distance
      v.; to take someone in a boat across a short distance

faker: n.; an imposter
fakir: n.; beggar

faro: n.; type of card game
farrow: n.; a litter of pigs
        v.; to give birth to piglets
pharaoh: n.; a ruler in ancient Egypt

fat: adj.; having a large amount of excess flesh
    n.; oily substance found in animals
phat: adj.; slang for excellent

fate: n.; events beyond one's control
    v.; be destined to happen
Fate: n.; one of three goddesses in mythology
fête: n.; a festival
    v.; to honor someone

faun: n.; part man, part goat in mythology
fawn: n.; a deer in its first year; a yellowish-brown color
    v.; to produce young deer

faux: adj.; not real; artificial or fake
foe: n.; enemy

favor: n.; approval, support, or liking for someone or something; an act of kindness beyond what is due or usual
    v.; to feel or show approval or preference for; to give someone something they want
favour: British spelling of favor

favorable: adj.; expressing approval; to the advantage of someone or something
favourable: adj.; British spelling of favorable

favorite: adj.; preferred above all others of the same type
    n.; person or thing well-liked by someone
favourite: British spelling of favorite

fay: n.; fairy or elf or sprite
Fay (or Faye): n.; a female name

faze: v.; to disturb or worry
phase: n.; a period or stage in a series of events or a process of development

feat: n.; a bold trick or stunt
feet: n.; plural of foot (lower part of leg upon which you walk)

fen: n; a low, marshy area of land
fin: n.; a fish's tail
Finn: n.; one from Finland, a Scandinavian country in Europe

fetal: adj.; relating to a fetus (an unborn baby of a mammal)
foetal: adj.; British spelling of fetal

fetus: n.; an unborn offspring of a mammal
foetus: n; British spelling of fetus

few: adj.; not many
phew: inter.; exclamation of relief

fiancé: n.; a man to whom one is going to marry
fiancée: n.; a woman to whom one is going to marry

fiber: n.; a thread or strand; a dietary material for digestion
fibre: n.; British spelling of fiber

fill: v.; to put something in a container in order to make it full
    n.; an amount which is as much as one wants
Phil: n.; a male first name, short for Phillip or Philip

filly: n.; a young female horse
Philly: n.; short name for Philadelphia, Pennsylvania

find: v.; to discover by chance; to discover something to be present
    n.; a discovery of something valuable
fined: v.; past tense of to fine (make one pay a sum of money)

finds: v.; discovers by chance
        n.; plural of find (a discovery)
fines: n.; plural of fine (a sum of money to be paid, especially after breaking the law)

finish: v.; to end or conclude
Finnish: adj.; having to do with Finland, a Scandinavian country in Europe

fir: n.; a type of evergreen tree
fur: n.; hair of animals

fish: n.; an animal that lives in the water and has fins and gills
        v.; try to catch fish; to try to find something; pull something out of the water
phish:v.; scam to get private information from internet users; to make someone a victim in this manner
        n.; the e-mail, for example, that tries to trick someone

fisher: n.; one who fishes for the cold-blooded animal in water
fissure: n.; a crack or split

flair: n.; a special talent for doing something well
flare: n.; sudden brief burst of light or flame; a gradual widening, as in skirts or pants
        v.; to burn or blaze suddenly
flayer: n.; one who flays (strips off skin or criticizes someone)

flak: n.; antiaircraft fire; strong disapproval
flack: n.; a publicity agent; another spelling of flak
        v.; to promote someone or something

flavor: n.; the taste of a food or drink
        v.; to change the taste of food or drink by adding something
flavour: British spelling of flavor

flea: n.; an insect
flee: v.; to run away or escape

flecks: n.; plural of fleck (small patch of color or light)
      v.; part of the verb to fleck (mark or dot with small patches of color or particles of something)
flex: v.; to bend
    n.; the act of flexing

flew: v.; past tense of fly (to move through the air using wings)
flu: n.; short for influenza, an illness
flue: n.; part of a chimney or fireplace where the smoke goes

Flo: n.; a female name, short for Florence
floe: n.; iceberg
flow: v.; to move along in a current or stream
    n.; the act of moving along a course

flocks: n.; plural of flock (a number of birds of one kind that are together)
phlox: n.; a type of flower

flour: n.; a powder used to make bread
    v.; to put flour on something
flower: n.; a plant, usually with colorful petals
    v.; to produce flowers or bloom

foaled: v.; past tense of foal (to give birth to a colt or filly)
fold: v.; to bend over on itself so that one part covers the other; to cover or wrap something
    n.; a form shaped by a draped piece of cloth

foe: n.; enemy
faux: adj.; not real (pronounced "fo" with long o)
pho: n.; type of Vietnamese soup

for: prep.; a word that indicates purpose or goal or the object of a desire or activity; because of; in place of; on behalf of; in favor of
  conj.; because
fore: adj.; placed in front
  n.; front part of something
  inter.; yelled as a warning to people in a golf ball's path
  prep.; a form of before
four: n.; the number 4

forbear: v.; keep from doing something
forebear: n.; an ancestor

fort: n.; a fortified building or permanent army post
forte: n.; something at which one excels

forth: adv.; ahead or forward; from this time forward
fourth: the number four in a series; one-fourth or a quarter of something

forward: adv.; toward the front or ahead; toward a good conclusion
  adj.; facing toward the front; related to the future
  n.; a player in a sport
  v.; to send on ahead; to promote
foreword: n.; an introduction to a book, usually by someone other than the author

foul: n.; in sports, an unfair strike
  v.; to make dirty or pollute; to commit a foul in a sport
  adj.; offensive or disgusting to the senses; wicked
  adv.; unfairly or against the rules
fowl: n.; a bird like a chicken, turkey, duck, or goose

franc: n.; the money unit of Switzerland, a country in Europe
frank: adj.; open and honest
Frank: n.; a male name, short for Franklin or Francis

frays: n.; plural of fray (a fight)
      v.; unravels or becomes worn, as in a fabric; shows the effects of stress; when a deer rubs its head on a tree
phrase: n.; a group of words
        v.; to put into a certain form of words

frees: v.; part of the verb to free (set at liberty or release from something)
freeze: v.; to turn into ice; store at a low temperature
      n.; the act of holding at a fixed state; period of very cold weather
frieze: n.; a type of art on a wall

friar: n.; member of a male religious order such as Dominican or Franciscan
fryer: n.; a type of container for frying food; a young chicken
      v.; one who fries food

fueled: v.; past tense of to fuel (to supply with fuel, such as coal, gas, or oil)
fuelled: v.; British spelling of fueled

furor: n.; anger or excitement
fuhrer (or fuehrer): n.; a horrible, ruthless leader

G

G: n.; the seventh letter of the alphabet
gee: n.; the letter G; a command to a horse to go faster or to turn right; one thousand dollars
     inter.; an exclamation of enthusiasm or sympathy

gaff: n.; a stick with a hook for catching large fish
     v.; to spear with a gaff
gaffe: n.; something causing embarrassment to the originator; a blunder

gage: n.; a measuring tool; a test of something
     v.; to measure; to judge a situation
guage: preferred spelling of gage

Gail (or Gale or Gayle): n.; a female name (Gale may be a male name)
Gael: n.; one who speaks Gaelic (especially the Celtic language of Scotland)
gale: n.; a strong wind

gait: n.; one's manner of walking; the pace of an animal, especially a horse
gate: n.; a hinged door

gall: n.; bold, shameless behavior; contents of gall bladder
Gaul: n.; a native of ancient Gaul in Western Europe

gamble: v.; to bet for money; take risky actions for a desired result
     n.; a bet
gambol: v.; to run and jump playfully
     n.; the act of running and jumping

gaol: n.; British spelling of jail
     v.; to put someone in gaol (jail)
gel: n.; a thick, sticky, mostly clear substance, especially in cosmetics and medicine
     v.; to set or become more solid; to begin to work well
jail: n.; a place to keep people who commit crimes
     v.; to put someone in jail
jell: v.; to set or congeal like jelly

gem: n.; a jewel
gym: n.; short for gymnasium (a building for sports)
Jim: n.; a male name, short for James

gene: n.; part of DNA that is the basic unit of heredity
Gene: n.; a male name
Jean (or Jeanne): n.; a female name

genes: n.; plural of gene (see above)
jeans: n.; pants made of denim

gest (or geste): n.; a story of adventure or romance
jest: n.; a joke
     v.; to speak in a joking way

ghee: n.; a type of butter
gi: n.; clothes worn in martial arts like judo and karate
gie: v.; Scottish form of give

gibe: n.; an insulting remark
     v.; to make an insulting remark
jibe: n.; another spelling of gibe

gild: v.; to cover something thinly with gold
gilled: adj.; having gills (breathing organs of fish)
guild: n.; a union of people to achieve a common goal

gilt: adj.; covered thinly with gold
    n.; gold put on in a thin layer
guilt: n.; wrongdoing or criminality
    v.; to make someone feel guilty, especially to make them do something

gin: n.; a type of alcohol; a type of card game; a machine to separate cotton from its seeds; machine to lift heavy weights; a trap to catch animals
    v.; to separate cotton from its seeds in a cotton gin
Jen: n.; a female name, short for Jennifer

glamor: n.; beauty or charm that is attractive
glamour: n.; British spelling of glamor

glutenous: adj.; of gluten (a substance in grains)
glutinous: adj.; sticky
gluttonous: adj.; eating and drinking too much

gnat: n.; a small insect that bites
Nat: n.; a male name, short for Nathaniel

gnome: n.; a legendary dwarf-like creature supposed to guard the earth's treasures underground; an ugly, small person
Nome: n.; a city in Alaska

gnu: n.; a type of antelope
knew: v.; past tense of know (to be aware of or to realize)
new: adj.; recent or untried for the first time
nu: n.; the thirteenth letter of the Greek alphabet

gnus: n.; plural of gnu (see above)
news: n.; a recent report or announcement

goaled: v.; part of the verb to goal (to achieve a result)
gold: n.; a yellow precious metal; deep yellow color

gofer: n.; slang for one who runs errands, from go for
gopher: n.; a type of rodent that digs holes; also a type of tortoise; alternate spelling of gofer

gored: v.; past tense of gore (stab with an animal horn)
gourd: n.; a large fruit with a hard skin
gourde: n.; monetary unit of Haiti

gorilla: n.; an ape
guerilla: n.; a member of a small group of resistance fighters

graft: n.; offshoot of a plant; piece of tissue transplanted surgically; corruption
       v.; insert a twig as a graft; transplant living tissue; to fasten or attach
graphed: v.; past tense of graph (to plot a picture showing relationships between things on a graph)

grate: v.; to cut into small pieces; to make an irritating, rasping sound
       n.; part of a fireplace
great: adj.; above average
       n.; a famous person, favorably
       adv.; excellently or very well

grater: n.; a device for grating; one who grates
greater: adj.; better than

gray: adj.; a color between black and white
       n.; a gray color
       v.; to become gray with age
grey: British spelling of gray

grays: v.; becomes gray
graze: v.; eat grass in a field

grease: n.; a thick, oily lubricant
Greece: n.; a country in Europe

grill: n.; a metal frame used to cook food over a fire; type of dental jewelry
      v.; to cook using a grill; to question one heavily
grille: n.; a screen of metal bars or wires for protection or ventilation; ornamental one at the front of an automobile

grip: v.; to hold tightly; to greatly affect someone
      n.; a tight hold
grippe: n.; old term for the flu

grisly: adj.; causing horror or gruesome
grizzly: n.; a type of brown bear
       adj.; gray-haired

groan: v.; to make a deep sound due to pain or despair; to make a low creaking sound due to applied weight
      n.; the sound made due to pain, despair, or applied weight
grown: v.; part of the verb to grow (increase in size)

grocer: n.; one who sells food
grosser: adj.; comparative form of gross (disgusting)
      n.; a movie that earns an amount of money

guessed: v.; past tense of guess (to estimate)
guest: n.; one invited to visit someone's home or to take part in a function

guise: n.; appearance, usually hiding something
guys: n.; plural of guy (a man)

H

hail: n.; frozen rain

     v.; to fall as frozen rain; to fall as in a large number of objects; to call out to get someone's attention; to signal to stop, as to a taxi; to come from a certain place

hale: adj.; healthy and strong

hell: n.; a place thought to be in some religions as one of evil and suffering, beneath the earth

     inter.; an expression of annoyance or surprise

hair: n.; the thin strands growing on animals' skins

hare: n.; a long-eared mammal that looks like a rabbit

Herr: n.; German form of Mr.

hairy: adj.; having much hair

Harry: n.; a male name

hall: n.; an area in a building from which rooms open; a corridor; a large room for events; a college or university building

haul: v.; to pull with force; to pull something behind something else

     n.; something stolen

handsome: adj.; good-looking

hansom: n.; two-wheeled, horse-drawn vehicle

hangar: n.; large building, especially for airplanes

     v.; to put in a hangar

hanger: n.; a shaped object with a hook at the top upon which to put clothes; one who hangs something

harbor: n.; port or dock for ships
       v.; keep in one's mind, secretly; give a home or shelter to
harbour: British spelling of harbor

hart: n.; a male deer
heart: n.; the organ in the body that pumps blood; the inner part of something
       v.; to love

hay: n.; mowed, dry grass
       v.; to cut and dry grass
hey: inter.; expression used to attract attention; hello or hi

hays: n.; plural of hay (see above)
       v.; cuts and dries grass
haze: n.; fog or mist; a confused state of mind
       v.; to abuse
Hayes: n.; a last name or a male name

heal: v.; to make healthy again
heel: n.; the back part of the foot
       v.; to put a heel on a shoe
       inter.; a command to a dog to walk closely behind its owner
he'll: contraction for he will or he shall
hill: n.; a raised area of land

hear: v.; to listen; to be informed of something
here: adv.; in this place
       inter.; used to attract one's attention; used to show one's presence at roll call

heard: v.; past tense of hear (see above)
herd: n.; a group of animals
       v.; to move people or animals in a particular direction; to look after livestock

hearty: adj.; loud and cheerful; a large amount (of food)
hardy: adj.; able to endure difficult conditions

heed: v.; to pay attention to
      n.; attention
he'd: contraction for he had or he would

heroin: n.; a type of drug
heroine: n.; a woman who is admired; the chief female character in a book, movie, or play who has good qualities

hew: v.; to cut or chop
hue: n.; color or tint
Hugh: n.; a male name

hi: inter.; hello
hie: v.; to hurry
high: adj.; tall; slang for intoxicated by alcohol or drugs; greater than normal
      adv.; to a high degree or highly; at or to a considerable height
      n.; an elevated place; the state of being high on drugs or alcohol; a happy moment
heigh: inter.; old-fashioned way to express cheerfulness

hide: v.; to keep out of sight or secret
      n.; skin of an animal
hied: v.; past tense of hie (to go quickly)
Hyde: n.; a surname (last name)

higher: comparative form of high (see above)
hire: v.; to employ someone
      n.; one who is hired

him: pron.; used as an object of a preposition or verb to refer to a male; he; that man
hem: n.; the edge of a piece of cloth, turned under and sewn
      v.; to put a hem on; to surround; to make a hesitating sound in the throat
hymn: n.; a religious song

ho: inter.; used to attract attention to something or someone

        n.; slang for whore or prostitute

hoe: n.; a garden tool used for weeding and breaking up ground

        v.; to use a hoe to dig

hoar: adj.; grayish-white

        n.; hoarfrost (a type of frost)

hoer: n; one who hoes (breaks up ground with a hoe)

whore: n.; a prostitute (also spelled hore)

        v.; to prostitute oneself

hoard: v.; to amass money or objects

        n.; a stock of money or objects, sometimes secretly stored

horde: n.; a large number of people

whored: v.; past tense of to whore (see above)

hoarse: adj.; sounding rough, as in one's voice

horse: n.; a large plant-eating mammal used for riding or pulling loads

hoes: n.; plural of hoe (see above)

        v.; part of the verb to hoe (see above)

hose: n.; a tube used to convey water; stockings or socks or tights

        v.; to water or spray with a hose

hold: v.; to support with one's arms or hands; to keep or detain someone

        n.; part of a ship for storage; the act of grasping something; power or control

holed: v.; past tense of to hole (to make a hole; hit a ball so that it falls in a hole)

hole: n.; a hollow place in a solid surface; a small, unpleasant place

        v.; to make a hole in; to hit a ball so it falls in a hole

whole: adj.; all of something

        n.; a thing that is complete in itself

holm: n.; an islet

hom: n.; a type of plant in India

home: n.; place where one lives; place where one needs professional care

adj.; of the place where one lives; of a sports game played at the team's own field or court

adv.; to or at the place where one lives

v.; relating to an animal that returns by instinct to a place after leaving it; aim toward

holy: adj.; sacred or blessed

holey: adj.; having holes

wholly: adv.; entirely or fully or altogether

honor: n.; great respect; morality

v.; to think highly of; to keep an agreement

honour: British spelling of honor

hostel: n.; a place to stay when out of town; an inn

hostile: adj.; unfriendly; of a military enemy; opposed to

hour: n.; 60 minutes

our: pron.; belonging to the speaker and one or more others; belonging to us

hours: n.; plural of hour (see above)

ours: pron.; belonging to the speaker and one or more others

humerus: n.; the long bone in an arm from the shoulder to the elbow

humorous: adj.; funny

humor: n.; quality of being funny; comedy; a state of mind

v.; to grant the wishes of someone to keep them happy

humour: British spelling of humor

I

I: n.; ninth letter of the English alphabet; Roman numeral for 1
I: pron.; myself
aye: inter.; yes
eye: n.; organ of sight
     v.; to look at closely

I'd: contraction for I would or I had or I should
eyed: v. past tense of to eye (see above)
     adj.; having eyes

idle: adj.; lazy and avoiding work; with no purpose; pointless
     v.; spend time doing nothing; run slowly, like an engine
idol: n.; image used as something to admire, love, or worship
idyll (or idyl): n.; a happy, peaceful scene

idolize: v.; admire or love greatly or excessively
idolise: v.; British spelling of idolize

I'll: contraction for I will or I shall
isle: n.; a small island
aisle: n.; a walkway between rows of seats

illicit: adj.; illegal
elicit: v.; to bring forth or draw out

illusion: n.; false impression
elusion: n.; hiding or escaping from someone

immerge: v.; to immerse oneself in something
emerge: v.; move away from something and come into view

immersed: v.; past tense of to immerse (to dip in a liquid); deeply involved in an interest
emersed: adj.; having to do with a plant reaching above the surface of the water

immersion: n.; plunging or dipping
emersion: n.; act of emerging from water

immigrant: n.; one who comes to live in a foreign country
emigrant: n.; one who leaves his or her own country to move to another

imminent: adj.; about to happen
immanent: adj.; existing within or essential or fundamental
eminent: adj.; of a famous and respected person with regard to a certain profession; clear or obvious

impassable: adj.; impossible to be traveled over
impassible: adj.; unable to feel pain

impressed: adj.; showing respect for someone or something
imprest: n.; an amount of money given to a person for some reason; petty cash

in: prep.; on the inside of or within
inn: n.; small hotel

incidence: n.; the rate of occurrence of something
incidents: n.; plural of incident (an event or occurrence)

incite: v.; to encourage or stir up, especially in a violent or illegal way
insight: n.; a deep understanding of someone or something

indict: v.; to charge with a crime
indite: v.; to write or compose

indiscreet: adj.; revealing things that should be secret
indiscrete: adj.; not divided into parts

ingenious: adj.; having the trait of being clever
ingenuous: adj.; being frank and candid

innocence: n.; state of being innocent (free from sin; chaste or pure; guiltless)
innocents: n.; plural of innocent (person who is childlike and honest)

insolent: adj.; showing a rude lack of respect
insulant: n.; an insulating material (one that protects something from loss of heat or too much sound)

instance: n.; an example or single occurrence of something
       v.; to cite a fact as an example
instants: n.; plural of instant (a moment in time)

insure: v.; arrange to be paid back in case of damage to property or injury or death
ensure: v.; make sure something will happen or be provided

intense: adj.; of extreme degree or strength; having or showing strong feelings
intents: n.; plural of intent (purpose)

intension: n.; determination
intention: n.; purpose or aim

invade: v.; to enter a region to occupy it
inveighed: v.; past tense of inveigh (to speak or write about something with rage or hostility)

islet: n.; a small island (silent s)
eyelet: n.; a small round hole in which to put a shoelace, for example

its: pron.; belonging to
it's: contraction for it is

J

J: n.; the tenth letter of the English alphabet
jay: n.; a type of bird, a bluejay; a person who talks a lot

jail: n.; prison
    v.; to put in a jail
gaol: n.; British spelling of jail

jam: n.; jelly or preserves; the act of getting stuck; an awkward situation; an informal gathering of musicians
    v.; to pack tightly in; to become stuck; to play informally with other musicians
jamb: n.; the side of a doorway or window

Jean (or Jeanne): n.; female name usually
gene: n.; a unit of heredity

jeans: n. pants, usually made of denim
genes: n.; plural of gene (see above)

jest: n.; a joke
    v.; to speak or act jokingly
geste or gest: n.; a notable deed or exploit

jibe: v.; to agree with; change course in sailing; to insult
    n.; an insult; being in agreement with
gibe: alternate spelling of jibe
(note: some dictionaries say jibe means agree and gibe means to insult)

Jim: n.; male name, short for James
gym: n.; short for gymnasium

Juan: n.; male name
wan: adj.; pale

judgment: n.; making a conclusion; bad luck seen as punishment
judgement: n.; British spelling of judgment although currently they prefer judgment

Juno: n.; a Roman goddess, wife of Jupiter
Juneau: n.; capital of Alaska

jury: n.; a number of people, usually 12, that give a verdict in court
Jewry: n.; the Jewish people

K

K: n.; the eleventh letter of the English alphabet; slang for okay
cay: n.; a low bank made of coral, rock or reef
Kay (or Kaye): n.; a female name, sometimes a nickname for Katherine or Kathleen
kay: slang for okay

karat: n.; the unit of fineness for gold
carat: n.; unit of weight to measure gems
caret: n.; a mark used to mean something is to be inserted
carrot: n.; a type of vegetable

keel: n.; bottom of a boat
     v.; to turn over or capsize; collapse
kill: v.; to cause the death of; to cause the failure of
     n.; an act of killing

kernel: n.; the center of a nut or seed
colonel: n.; an officer in the army

keto: adj.; relating to ketone (in chemistry, an organic compound); ketogenic, or keto low-carb, high-fat diet
Quito: n.; the capital of Ecuador in South America

key: n.; a small piece of metal shaped to fit in a lock to open or close it; the buttons on a computer or typewriter or telephone
     adj.; central or important
     v.; to enter data by means of a keyboard
 quay: n.; a dock or wharf or pier

khan: n.; title given to rulers in Asia
con: v.; to cheat
      n.; the deceiving of someone; disadvantage; short for convict
Cannes: n; city in France

kilometer: n.; 1000 meters or 0.62 mile
kilometre: n.; alternate spelling of kilometer

knave: n.; a dishonest and bad man; another name for the jack in a deck of cards
nave: n.; central part of a church

knead: v.; to work into dough, especially for bread; to massage or squeeze
kneed: v.; past tense of to knee (to hit with one's knee)
      adj.; having knees
need: v.; to require something important
      n.; a thing that is wanted or required; the state of requiring help

kneel: v.; to fall to one's knees (the joint between the thigh and lower leg in humans)
Neil (or Neal): n.; a male name
nil: n.; zero
    adj.; nonexistent

knell: v.; to ring solemnly, especially for a death
      n.; the sound of a bell, especially for a death
Nell: n.; female name

knew: v.; past tense of know (to be aware of or realize)
new: adj.; not existing before; already existing but seen for the first time
      adv.; recently
gnu: n.; a type of antelope

knight: n.; in the Middle Ages, a man who served his lord as a soldier in armor
      v.; to bestow the title of knight on someone
night: n.; the time from sunset to sunrise; the evening

knit: v.; to sew with yarn; to unite
     n.; a knitted fabric
nit: n.; the egg or young of a louse (singular of lice)

knob: n.; a round ball on something; handle on a door or drawer; button for adjusting a machine
nob: n.; a wealthy person; a person's head

knot: n.; a fastening made by tying rope or string, for example; a tangle in something; a hard lump on a tree; an unpleasant feeling in a part of the body; a unit of speed equal to one nautical mile per hour
     v.; to fasten with a knot; to make tangled; to cause to tighten from nervousness
not: adv.; used with a helping verb or a form of "to be" to form the negative

know: v.; to be aware of; to be acquainted with
     n.; an awareness of
no: adj.; not any
    inter.; opposite of yes, said excitedly
    adv.; not at all
    n.; a negative answer
Noh: n.; A Japanese masked drama with song and dance

knows: v.; part of the verb to know (see above)
noes: n.; plural of no (see above)
nose: n.; part of the body used for breathing and smelling; front end of an aircraft, etc.; a sense of smell; gift for detecting something; the smell of something, especially wine
     v.; to push one's nose against something; to investigate something; to make one's way forward slowly; to be leading by a small margin

L

L: n.; the twelfth letter of the English alphabet; Roman numeral for 50
ell: n.; the letter L; a measurement, about 45 inches; extension of a building
that is shaped like an L; L-shaped connector of pipes
el: n.; short for elevated railroad

labor: n.; work, especially hard and physical; process of childbirth
      v.; to work hard; to struggle against; to be in labor (childbirth)
labour: n.; British spelling of labor

lacks: n.; plural of lack (state of being without or not having enough)
      v.; is without or deficient in
lax: adj.; not strict or severe or careful enough; relaxed

laid: v.; past tense of lay (to put or place)
lade: v.; to load a ship

lain: v.; part of the verb to lie (to rest or recline)
lane: n.; a narrow road; a part of a road

lair: n.; a wild animal's den; a person's secret place
layer: n.; usually one of several thicknesses of material covering a surface;
one who lays something

lam: n.; the running away from police
      v.; to hit; to run to try to escape
lamb: n.; a baby sheep

lama: n.; a title of a spiritual leader of Tibet in Inner Asia
llama: n.; a pack animal in the camel family

laps: n.; plural of lap (the area between the waist and knees of someone who is sitting down); plural of a stage in track or swimming
lapse: n.; a passage of time
      v.; to expire; to pass slowly into
Lapps: n.; plural of Lapp (member of a people of Scandinavia)

lay: v.; to put or place down
      n.; the general look of a place; poem meant to be sung
     adj.; not belonging to the clergy; not having expert knowledge, especially in medicine or law
lei: n.; a Polynesian wreath of flowers
ley: n.; area of land used as a temporary pasture for animals

lays: v.; part of the verb to lay (see above)
      n.; plural of lay (poem meant to be sung)
lase: v.; function as or in a laser (a device that makes an intense beam of light)
laze: v.; spend a relaxing time
      n.; an amount of time being lazy

lea: n.; a grassy area or meadow
lee: n.; the side away from wind
Lee: n.; a male name or a surname
Leigh: n.; a female name

leach: v.; to drain
leech: n.; a type of bloodsucking worm

lead: n.; a type of metal
led: v.; past tense of to lead (to guide or show someone the way)

leaf: n.; usually a green, flat, blade-like part of a plant or tree
      v.; put out new leaves (plural of leaf)
Leif: n.; a male name
lief: adv.; happily

leak: n.; a hole in something through which liquid accidentally passes; an intentional telling of a secret
    v.; to accidentally lose contents through a hole or crack; to become known, as a secret
leek: n.; a type of onion

lean: adj.; not fat
    v.; to be in a sloping position
    n.; an inclination
lien: n.; the right to possess property of another until a debt is paid

leased: v.; past tense of to lease (to rent)
least: adv.; the smallest degree
    adj.; the smallest amount

leaver: n.; one who leaves a place or position
lever: n.; a crowbar, one of the 6 simple machines
    v.; to lift with a lever

lends: v.; part of the verb to lend (to give one the use of something that must be returned)
lens: n.; the light-gathering part of a camera or eye

lessen: v.; to diminish or grow smaller
lesson: n.; a period of learning; something learned by experience

levee: n.; a ridge built to prevent overflow from a river
levy: v.; to charge a tax on something
    n.; the act of levying a tax or fee or fine

liable: adj.; legally responsible for; likely to do or be something; likely to experience something bad
libel: n.; a published false statement damaging one's reputation
    v.; to defame someone in writing

liar: n.; one who lies (tells untruths)
lier: n.; one who rests or reclines
lyre: n.; a small, stringed musical instrument

license: n.; permit to own or use or do something
v.; to give a license to someone or something
licence: British spelling of license

lichen: n.; a type of plant that grows on rocks, trees, or walls
liken: v.; to compare

licker: n.; one who licks (passes the tongue over something)
liquor: n.; alcoholic drinks

lie: n.; an untruth; the way in which something lies
v.; to be in a horizontal resting position; to be in a certain state
lye: n.; a strong solution used for cleaning

lieu: n.; instead; in place of
loo: n.; British for bathroom or toilet
Lou: n.; a name

lightening: n.; a stage of pregnancy
v.; making lighter in weight; a brightening
lightning: n.; electrical current within a cloud or between the earth and a cloud
adj.; very fast

limb: n.; an arm or leg; branch of a tree
limn: v.; to describe in words or a painting

links: n.; a golf course; plural of link (connection or relationship or part of a chain)
v.; joins
lynx: n.; a type of wild cat

liter: n.; a metric unit of volume, about 1.75 pints or one cubic decimeter or a little more than a quart
litre: alternate spelling of liter

lo: inter.; used to draw attention to something amazing
low: adj.; less than average height or the opposite of high; below average in amount

n.; a low point; at the bottom of something; sound made by a cow
adv.; in a low position or state
v.; of a cow, to moo

load: n.; cargo or freight; a weight on something; a lot of something
      v.; put a load of something on or in; take, buy, or eat a lot of; to put ammunition in a firearm
lode: n.; a rich source of something, especially metal ore
lowed: v.; past tense of to low (to make the sound of a cow)

loan: n.; something borrowed, especially money, to be paid back with interest
      v.; to lend something
lone: adj.; solitary or solo; isolated

loath: adj.; unwilling or reluctant to do something
loathe: v.; to hate
loth: adj.; alternate spelling of loath

locks: n.; plural of lock (a fastener for a door or lid; part of a canal; piece of hair)
      v.; fastens with a lock or restricts access to
lox: n.; smoked salmon; short for liquid oxygen

Loki: n.; a Norse god in mythology
low-key: adj.; not showy; modest

loop: n.; shape made by a curve that goes around and crosses itself
      v.; form something into a loop
loupe: n.; a small magnifying glass used by jewelers and watchmakers

loot: n.; things taken from an enemy
      v.; to steal things
lute: n.; a type of stringed instrument

luster: n.; shine
lustre: n.; British spelling of luster

M

M: n.; the thirteenth letter of the English alphabet; Roman numeral for 1000
em: n.; the letter M; a measurement used in printing

ma: n.; short for mama or mom; mother
maw: n.; stomach; the throat of a animal who eats great amounts of food; a gaping mouth

madam: n.; a respectful way to address a woman
madame: n.; French spelling of madam

made: v.; past tense of make (to form by putting parts together; to create)
       adj.; formed in a certain place or by a certain process
maid: n.; a female servant; a young woman, especially an unmarried virgin

magnate: n.; a rich, important person, especially in business
magnet: n.; a piece of iron that attracts other objects containing iron; a person or thing with a strong attraction

mail: n.; letters and packages
     v.; to send a letter or package
male: n.; a masculine person, plant, or animal
     adj.; to do with men

maim: v.; to injure a part of the body permanently
Mame: n.; a female name

main: adj.; most important
       n.; a principal pipe carrying water or gas
mane: n.; the long hair growing on the neck of an animal
Maine: n.; a state in New England
mein: n.; Chinese noodles

maize: n.; corn
maze: n.; a puzzle of paths and hedges in which one has to find a way out

Malay: n.; person living in Malaysia and Indonesia
melee: n.; a fight or disturbance or commotion; a confused mass of people

mall: n.; a large building with many stores
maul: v.; to hurt by scratching or tearing
       n.; a type of hammer-like tool
moll: n.; a gangster's female companion; a prostitute

maneuver: n.; a movement that needs skill; a large-scale military exercise
       v.; to move skillfully or carefully
manoeuvre: from the French, but the British spelling of maneuver

manner: n.; the way in which something is done; one's way of behaving toward others
manor: n.; a large country house with land

mantel: n.; the beam or ledge above a fireplace
mantle: n.; a cloak or cape; responsibility passing from one to another
       v.; to clothe in a mantle

mare: n.; a female horse or other equine
mayor: n.; the head of a city or town

marquee: n.; a tall projection above a theater, usually telling the name of the play or film, etc.
marquis: n.; a nobleman ranking above a count and below a duke

marry: v.; to wed; to combine
Mary: n.; a female name
merry: adj.; happy or cheerful

marshal: n.; a high-ranking officer in the armed forces; a federal law officer
          v.; arrange people, especially soldiers, in order
marshall: n.; British spelling of marshal
Marshall: n.; a name
martial: adj.; pertaining to war or the military

marten: n.; a weasel-like mammal
martin: n.; a type of bird
Martin: n.; a name

mask: n.; a covering for the face, as a disguise; a covering for the mouth and nose
          v.; to cover with a mask; to hide something
masque: n.; entertainment in 16th and 17th century England with dancing and acting by masked players; another spelling of mask

massed: v.; past tense of to mass (to assemble as one body or gather together)
mast: n.; part of a sailboat; court of the Navy to hear cases of minor offenses by the captain

mat: n.; piece of coarse material to wipe your feet on or a piece of paper, cork, etc., placed on a table to protect it; thick layer of hair
          v.; to tangle, as in hair
matte: adj.; without a shine, as on a photograph
          n.; a matte paint or finish; a mount or border around a picture; also another spelling of mat
          v.; give a matte appearance to something
Mat or Matt: n.; nickname for Matthew or Mateo

may: v.; expressing possibility or permission; expressing a wish or a hope
          n.; the hawthorn bush or its blossom
May: n.; the fifth month of the year; a surname or a female first name
meh: inter.; expressing a lack of excitement or enthusiasm
          adj.; uninspiring or boring
Mae: n; a female name

me: pron.; myself
mi: n.; the third note of the musical scale; me in Spanish

mead: n.; an alcoholic drink with honey and water
Mede: n.; a native of ancient Media in Persia (Iran today)
meed: n.; a deserved share or reward

meager: adj.; of something provided, short in quantity or quality
meagre: adj.; British spelling of meager

meal: n.; food eaten regularly
mil: n.; a unit of length, one-thousandth of an inch; a milliliter
mill: n.; a factory for grinding grain into flour or for other manufacturing processes
     v.; to grind something in a mill

mean: v.; to indicate or express or suggest
     adj.; unkind
     n.; the average, taken by adding numbers and then dividing by the number of numbers given
mesne: adj.; in law, intermediate
mien: n.; one's look and manner; appearance

meant: v.; past tense of to mean (to signify or convey or indicate)
mint: n.; a plant used as an herb; a peppermint candy; place where money is made; a large sum of money
     adj.; in new condition
     v.; to make a coin; produce for the first time

meat: n.; the flesh of an animal as food
meet: v.; to make contact with someone or come face to face with; touch or join
     n.; a sporting event
mete: v.; to distribute

medal: n.; a metal badge awarded to someone special
     v.; to earn a medal
meddle: v.; to interfere with something that is not one's business
metal: n.; a solid material, usually hard and shiny and mined from the earth
mettle: n.; one's coping ability in difficult situations

meeting: n.; an assemblage of people
        v.; part of the verb to meet (see above); making the acquaintance of someone for the first time; touching or joining; fulfilling or satisfying
meting: v.; part of the verb to mete (to apportion or allot)

memorialize: v.; to preserve the memory of
memorialise: v.; British spelling of memorialize

memorize: v.; to commit to memory or learn by heart
memorise: v.; British spelling of memorize

meter: n.; unit of length in the metric system, 100 centimeters or about 39.37 inches
metre: alternate spelling of meter

mew: n.; a high-pitched crying noise made by a cat usually
        v.; to meow, especially like a cat
mu: n.; the twelfth letter of the Greek alphabet

mewl: v.; cry or whimper, especially like a baby
mule: n.; the offspring of a male donkey and a female horse; a carrier of illegal drugs

mews: n.; plural of mew (see above)
muse: n.; something that is a source of inspiration for an artist; one of nine goddesses of arts and sciences in mythology; a period of thought or reflection
        v.; to be absorbed in thought

might: v.; past tense of may (expressing possibility or permission)
        n.; great strength
mite: n.; a very small arachnid, related to ticks

milk: n.; white fluid rich in fat and protein, secreted by female mammals for the nourishment of their young
        v.; to draw milk from an animal; to steal small amounts of money over a period of time
milque (toast): n.; a timid person who is easily dominated

mince: v.; grind food into small pieces
mints: n.; plural of mint (a type of herb or also a peppermint candy)

mind: n.; brain
      v.; be annoyed by or feel concern about
mined: v.; past tense of to mine (to obtain a mineral from a mine in the earth)

miner: n.; one who works in a mine
minor: n.; an under-age person; in music, a minor key
      adj.; lesser in importance
      v.; study a second subject in school

minks: n.; plural of mink (an animal valued for its fur)
minx: n.; a bold, flirty woman

missal: n.; a book containing Catholic texts
missile: n.; a type of weapon propelled at a target

missed: v.; past tense of to miss (to fail to hit or notice)
mist: n.; haze or fog
      v.; to cover with mist
Myst: n.; a computer game

moan: n.; a long, low sound made by one experiencing pain or pleasure
      v.; to make the sound of a moan
mown: adj.; cut down, as of grass
      v.; part of the verb to mow (cut down)

moat: n.; a deep and wide ditch especially around a castle for protection
      v.; to surround with a moat
mote: n.; a tiny speck of a substance

mode: n.; how something happens or is done; a style; the number occurring most often in a set of data
mowed: v.; past tense of to mow (cut down, as in grass)

mold: n.; a container used to make a shape; a style or form
v.; to form an object into a certain shape
mould: alternate spelling of mold

mooch: v.; to ask for something without paying for it
n.; one who mooches
mouch: British spelling of mooch

moor: n.; an area of uncultivated upland
more: adj.; greater amount
Moore: n.; a last name

moose: n.; a type of large deer
mousse: n.; a type of dessert; a bunch of bubbles on top of wine; a styling product for hair
v.; to style hair with mousse

moralize: v.; comment on the right and wrong of something
moralise: v.; British spelling of moralize

morn: n.; morning
mourn: v.; to feel or show sadness, especially for the death of someone

morning: n.; the time between midnight and noon
mourning: n.; the expressing of great sorrow for one who has died; black clothes worn to express grief when someone dies

mucous: adj.; relating to mucus
mucus: n.; a slimy substance from mucous membranes inside the nose

Mrs.: n.; a title for a married woman, short for mistress
misses: n.; plural of miss (usually an unmarried woman)

muscat: n.; a type of grape or a wine made from muscat grapes
Muscat: n.; capital of Oman in the Middle East
musket: n.; a type of old gun

muscle: n.; fibrous tissue in a body to help produce movement; physical strength
        v.; to move something with physical strength
mussel: n.; a type of bivalve mollusk found in the sea

mustard: n.; a tart yellow or brown paste used as a condiment on food
mustered: v.; past tense of to muster (to assemble, especially troops)

N

N: n.; the fourteenth letter of the alphabet
en: n.; the letter N; a measurement in printing

nae: Scottish no or not
nay: adv.; or rather; and more than that; no
      n.; a negative answer or vote
née: adj.; originally named; born
neigh: n.; a high-pitched sound made by a horse
      v.; especially of a horse, to make a high-pitched sound

nap: n.; a short sleep
      v.; to take a short sleep
nappe: n.; a sheet of rock that has moved sideways; the desired consistency of sauce
knap: n.; the top of a hill or mountain

Nat: n.; a male name
gnat: n.; a small, biting insect

naught: n.; 0 or zero
      pron.; old-fashioned word for nothing
nought: another spelling of naught

naval: adj.; relating to a navy
navel: n.; the place in a belly where the umbilical cord was; the center of a place

nave: n.; the central part of a church
knave: n.; old-fashioned term for a dishonest man; another term for the jack in cards

Neal (or Neil): n.; a male name
nil: n.; zero, especially in sports
    adj.; nonexistent
kneel: v.; fall to one's knees

necklace: n.; a chain or string of beads, etc., worn around the neck
neckless: adj.; having no neck (the part of the body that connects the head and the rest of the body, or a narrow part of something)

need: v.; require something
    n.; necessity
knead: v.; work into dough to make bread; squeeze with the hands
kneed: v.; past tense of to knee (to hit someone or something with one's knee)

neighbor: n.; person living near or next door to you
    v.; to be next to or very near
neighbour: British spelling of neighbor

Nell: n.; a female name
knell: n.; the sound of a bell, especially rung for a death
    v.; of a bell, to ring solemnly

new: adj.; not existing before; already existing but seen for the first time
knew: v.; past tense of to know (to be aware of or to realize)
gnu: n.; an African antelope
nu: n.; the thirteenth letter of the Greek alphabet

nice: adj.; pleasant or kind
gneiss: n.; a type of rock

nicks: n.; plural of nick (a little cut); British slang for prison
    v.; part of the verb to nick (make a small cut in); slang for steal, cheat, or arrest; slang for go fast or go away
nix: v.; put an end to
    pron.; nothing
    inter.; a refusal

niece: n.; the daughter of one's brother or sister or one's bother-in-law or sister-in-law
Nice: n.; city in France

night: n.; the time from sunset to sunrise
knight: n.; in the Middle Ages, a man who served his lord as a soldier in armor on horseback
      v.; to bestow the title of knight on someone

nit: n.; the egg or young of a louse
knit: v.; to make a blanket or piece of clothing by interlocking yarn or wool; to cause to unite

no: adv.; not at all; not any; a negative response
know: v.; be aware of or realize; develop a relationship with

nob: n.; a wealthy person or one high in social position; a person's head
knob: n.; a round handle of a drawer or door; a round lump, especially at the end or on top of something; a button for controlling a machine

Nome: n.; a seaport city in Alaska
gnome: n.; troll; dwarfish creature

none: pron.; not any
      adv.; not at all; by no amount
nun: n.; a religious woman of poverty and chastity, also called a sister

nose: n.; part of the face for breathing and smelling
      v.; to push against; to pry into something
noes: n.; plural of no
knows: v.; part of the verb to know (see above)

not: adv.; used with a helping verb or form of "to be" to form the negative; a short substitute for a negative clause
knot: n.; a fastening made by tying string, rope, etc.
      v.; to fasten with a knot; to make tangled

O

O!: inter.; another spelling of oh; used before a name in direct address, especially in poetry and prayer
oh: inter.; another spelling of O
owe: v.; have an obligation to pay in return for something received
eau: n.; French for water; perfume or cologne

oar: n.; a pole with a flat blade for rowing a boat
    v.; to row or propel through water
o'er: adv. or prep.; poetic for over
or: conj.; used to indicate an alternative
ore: n.; a natural solid material in the earth from which valuable metal is extracted

ode: n.; a lyric poem addressing a certain subject
owed: v.; past tense of to owe (see above)

odor: n.; a smell, especially bad
odour: British spelling of odor

offal: n.; trash or rubbish or waste
awful: adj.; unpleasant or bad

offed: v.; past tense of off (to kill)
oft: adv.; poetic for often

offense: n.; an illegal act; annoyance or resentment; action of attacking; in sports, possessing the ball
offence: British spelling of offense

old: adj.; having lived a long time; not young; former or previous
olde: adj.; alternate spelling of old to show quaintness

oleo: n.; margarine
olio: n.; a miscellaneous collection of things; a type of stew in Spain and Portugal

one: n.; the number 1
      pron.; referring to a before-mentioned person or thing; a person of a specific kind
won: v.; past tense of to win (to be successful in something)

oracle: n.; one acting as a medium through which advice or prophecy is sought; the place where such a prophecy was sought; the message given by an oracle
auricle: n.; part of the heart; something resembling an ear

oral: adj.; spoken; relating to the mouth
      n.; a spoken test
aural: adj.; having to do with the ear or hearing

ordinance: n.; a law
ordnance: n.; guns or artillery or a branch of the military that deals with weapons

organization: n.; an organized body of people with a certain purpose; the act of organizing something
organisation: n.; British spelling of organization

organize: v.; to put in order; prepare for an event
organise: v.; British spelling of organize

oriel: n.; type of bay window
oriole: n.; type of bird
aureole: n.; a circle of light around something's head, especially in art depicting holiness; another word for areola (a small, circular area of pigmented skin around a nipple)

our: pron.; belonging to the speaker and one or more people
hour: n.; 60 minutes; one twenty-fourth of a day

ours: pron.; used to refer to a thing or things belonging to the speaker and one or more other people
hours: n.; plural of hour (see above)

P

P: n.; the sixteenth letter of the English alphabet
pea: n.; a vegetable
pee: n.; the letter P; slang for urine
    v.; slang for to urinate

pa: n.; short for papa; dad or daddy; father
paw: n.; an animal's foot
    v.; to feel with a paw or hoof

paced: v.; past tense of to pace (to walk back and forth)
paste: n.; adhesive or glue; a mixture of a dry substance with liquid
    v.; to coat with paste

packed: v.; past tense of to pack (to fill with items needed while away from home)
    adj.; wrapped or loaded
pact: n.; a treaty or agreement or contract

paean: n.; a song of praise or triumph
paeon: n.; a metrical foot of one long syllable and three short ones in any order
pean: n.; type of fur
peon: n.; a Spanish-American day laborer; in Asia, a low-ranking laborer or soldier

pail: n.; bucket
pale: adj.; light in color; weak and unimpressive
    v.; to whiten; seem less important
pell: v.; old term for to beat or pelt

pain: n.; physical suffering; great effort
    v.; to cause physical or mental pain
pane: n.; window glass; a sheet of postage stamps

pair: n.; set of two things
    v.; to connect together to form a pair
pare: v.; to peel; to cut off outer edges; to reduce or decrease
pear: n.; type of fruit

palate: n.; the roof of the mouth; one's appreciation of sophisticated taste
palette: n.; the board upon which an artist mixes color; range of colors or tones used by an artist or musician
pallet: n.; a makeshift bed; a platform on which things can be moved or stored

pall: n.; a funeral cloth; a dark cloud of dust or smoke
    v.; become less interesting
Paul: n.; a male name

palm: n.; a type of tree; the inner part of a hand
    v.; to hide, especially as part of a trick; hit something with the palm of the hands
pom: n.; part of pom pom (or pompon), a group of streamers waved by cheerleaders

paralyze: v.; cause to become unable to move or think or act normally
paralyse: v.; British spelling of paralyze

parlay: v.; to turn previous winnings into a greater amount by gambling
    n.; a series of bets in which past winnings are used in other bets
parley: n.; a talk between opposite sides in a dispute
    v.; to talk with an opposing side to discuss terms

parlor: n.; a sitting room in a private house or a room in a public building for seeing guests
parlour: British spelling of parlor

passed: v.; past tense of to pass (to move in a certain direction or to go past or across)
past: adj.; earlier or long ago
      n.; time before the moment of writing or speaking
      prep.; to or on the farther side of
      adv.; so as to pass from one side to the other; used to show a time lapse

patience: n.; ability to accept delay or problems without getting upset
patients: n.; plural of patient (one receiving medical treatment)

patronize: v.; to treat in a way that seems nice but also gives the feeling of superiority; to frequent a place as a customer
patronise: v.; British spelling of patronize

pause: v.; to stop briefly
      n.; a temporary stop in action
paws: n.; plural of paw (an animal's foot)

peace: n.; tranquility or calm; period of no war
piece: n.; part of something
      v.; to put something together

pediatric: adj.; relating to the branch of medicine dealing with children
paediatric: adj.; British spelling of pediatric

peak: n.; the pointed top of a mountain
      v.; to reach a highest point
      adj.; maximum or greatest
peek: v.; to look quickly or spy
      n.; a quick look
pique: n.; a feeling of irritation resulting from hurt pride
      v.; stir up interest

peal: v.; to ring loudly
      n.; loud ringing of a bell; loud laughter
peel: v.; remove the outer covering
      n.; the outer covering of a fruit or vegetable
pill: n.; a small tablet or capsule of medicine; a birth-control pill; slang for an unpleasant person

pearl: n.; hard material formed in an oyster that is a desired gem; a person or thing of great worth
purl: adj.; relating to a knitting stitch
      v.; to knit with a purl stitch
      n.; twisted silver or gold wire for a border
Perl: n.; a type of computer-programming language

peat: n.; a brown soil-like deposit, formed by decomposition and used for fuel or gardening
Pete: n.; a male name, short for Peter

pedal: n.; one of a pair used for powering a bicycle, etc.; a foot-operated mechanism in a motor vehicle
      v.; move by using pedals
peddle: v.; to sell by going place to place; to promote widely

peer: v.; to look closely
pier: n.; a dock or wharf

pen: n.; instrument for writing and drawing; an enclosure for animals
      v.; to write; to keep animals in a pen; confine one in a restricted space
pin: n.; a thin piece of metal with a sharp point on one end, used to fasten pieces of cloth
      v.; to fasten with a pin

penalize: v.; subject to punishment
penalise: v.; British spelling of penalize

penance: n.; self-punishment for doing wrong; the confession of sins and giving of absolution
      v.; to impose penance
pennants: n.; plural of pennant (a tapering flag on a ship or having to do with sports)

pend: v.; to remain undecided; to hang
penned: v.; past tense of to pen (write or compose)
      adj.; enclosed or caged

pendant: n.; jewelry hanging from a chain worn on the neck
        adj.; hanging down
pendent: adj.; overhanging or suspended; remaining undetermined

penitence: n.; showing sorrow for wrong-doing; repentance
penitents: n.; plural of penitent (one who repents his or her sins and asks forgiveness)

per: prep.; for each; by means of or in accordance with
purr: v.; make a low, continuous sound of contentment, especially of a cat
        n.; a low, continuous sound

perches: n.; plural of perch (thing on which a bird rests; a type of fish)
purchase: v.; to buy
        n.; something bought

personalize: v.; to make something according to certain requirements
personalise: v.; British spelling of personalize

petrel: n.; a type of seabird
petrol: n.; British for gasoline

pharaoh: n.; ancient Egyptian king
faro: n.; type of card game with gambling

phase: n.; period in a set of events or a process of development; each of the aspects of the moon
        v.; carry out in gradual stages
fays: n.; plural of fay (a fairy)
faze: v.; to disturb someone

phew: inter.; used to show relief
few: adj.; not many

phi: n.; the twenty-first letter of the Greek alphabet (may also be pronounced "fee")
fie: inter.; used to show disgust

phlox: n.; a type of flower
flocks: n.; plural of flock (birds or other animals of one kind that stay together)

photo: n.; short for photograph, a picture taken with a camera
　　　　v.; to take a photograph
　　　　adj.; photographic
foto: slang for photo

phrase: n.; a group of words
　　　　v.; put into words a certain way
frays: n.; plural of fray (a fight)

pi: n.; the sixteenth letter of the Greek alphabet; the ratio of the circumference of a circle to its diameter, approximately 3.14159
pie: n.; pastry; pizza

picture: n.; a drawing or painting
　　　　v.; to represent in a picture
pitcher: n.; a container for pouring liquids; the player who throws the ball to the batter

piece: n.; a part
　　　　v.; to put something together from parts
peace: n.; calmness and quiet; no war

pier: n.; wharf or dock
peer: v.; to look closely
　　　　n.; a contemporary

Pilate: n.; the Roman who ordered Jesus to be crucified
pilot: n.; one who operates an aircraft; a television show made to test an audience's reaction
  adj.; done as an experiment
  v.; act as a pilot of an aircraft; test something before introducing it more widely

pistil: n.; female part of a flower
pistol: n.; a small firearm; an energetic person

plain: adj.; simple and not decorated elaborately; of a person, not remarkable or special
  adv.; clearly
  n.; large area of flat land with few trees
plane: n.; a flat surface; level of existence; short for airplane; a type of tool
  adj.; completely flat
  v.; glide; travel in an airplane; to smooth wood with a plane

plait: n.; a braid
  v.; form into a plait
plat: n.; a plot of land
  v.; to map out a site for construction
platte: n.; a river system in the United States, North and South Platte Rivers

pleas: n.; plural of plea (an urgent request or a formal statement on behalf of a prisoner)
please: v.; to cause to be happy
  adv.; used in polite requests

pliers: n.; a type of tool for gripping or bending
plyers: n.; plural of plyer (one who plies (works with or at; provides with food and drink; directs many questions at))

plow: n.; a piece of farm equipment to make rows for planting; type of yoga pose
  v.; to turn over the earth with a plow to get ready to plant seeds; move in a fast, out-of-control way
plough: British spelling of plow

plum: n.; type of fruit
      adj.; a highly desirable goal
plumb: v.; measure the depth of water; test a vertical surface
      adj.; vertical and straight

Po: n.; longest river in Italy, a country in Europe
Poe: n.; Edgar Allan Poe, American writer known for his poetry and horror stories

point: n.; sharp end of a tool, weapon, or other object; a period in punctuation
      v.; direct one's attention to something by extending one's finger or something held in one's hand; put forward a fact as evidence
pointe: n.; the tips of the toes of ballet shoes or a dance performed on the tips of toes

pole: n.; a long, slender piece of wood or metal
      v.; to propel a boat with a pole
Pole: n.; a native of Poland
poll: n.; voting in an election
      v.; to ask the opinion of

pompom: n.; a small, woolen ball attached to a garment, especially a hat; a large group of colored streamers used by cheerleaders
pompon: n.; alternate spelling of pompom

poor: adj.; not rich; of an inferior quality
pore: n.; very small opening in the skin
      v.; to ponder or think deeply about
pour: v.; flow rapidly and steadily, as in liquid; to cause to flow from a container; to prepare and serve a drink; to fall heavily, as in rain; of people or things, to come or go in large numbers

populace: n.; people living in a certain area
populous: adj.; densely populated

pored: v.; past tense of pore (be absorbed in reading or thought)
poured: v.; past tense of pour (cause a liquid to flow from a container); fall heavily, like rain; donate in large amounts, like money; express one's feelings openly)

poser: n.; one who acts in a manner to impress others
poseur: n.; British spelling of poser

practice: n.; the action or use of; expected way of doing something
        v.; to do over and over; put into practice
practise: British spelling of practice

praise: v.; to express approval or admiration
        n.; the expression of approval or admiration
prays: v.; part of the verb to pray (to express thanks or a request to an object of worship; to wish or hope for something)
preys: v.; part of the verb to prey (to hunt and kill for food)
        n.; plural of prey (an animal that is hunted and killed by another for food)

premier: adj.; first or foremost or primary
        n.; a head of government
premiere: n.; the first performance of an artistic work like a movie or play
        v.; to give the first performance of

presence: n.; the state of occurring or being present in a place or thing
presents: n.; plural of present (something given to someone as a gift)

pretense: n.; trying to make something seem true that is not true
pretence: British spelling of pretense

pride: n.; a feeling of satisfaction of one's achievements
        v.; to be proud of
pried: v.; past tense of to pry (to inquire too closely into someone's private business; to move or lift something by pressing a tool against a fixed point)

prier: n.; one who pries into someone else's affairs; one who moves something with a tool
prior: adj.; coming before in time or previous

pries: v.; part of the verb to pry (inquire too closely into one's business; to move something with a tool)
prise: v.; use force to move, separate, or open something; get something from someone with difficulty; note: the first two seem to be used interchangeably
prize: n.; an award or reward
        adj.; something apt to be awarded a prize
        v.; to value highly

primer: n.; a textbook used to teach children to read
primmer: adj.; more proper or formal

prince: n.; the son of a king or queen
prints: n.; plural of print (text in books, etc.; mark left on a surface due to pressure, as in hand or foot)

princes: n.; plural of prince (the son of a king or queen)
princess: n.; the daughter of a king or queen

principal: adj.; main or primary; denoting a sum of money originally invested or lent
        n.; the most important person; an amount of money invested or lent
principle: n.; an important truth or concept or idea

profit: n.; a financial gain
        v.; to make a financial gain, especially from an investment
prophet: n.; seer or forecaster of the future

program: n.; planned events; details of an event; instructions to a computer; a presentation of events

       v.; write a computer program; cause a person or animal to act in a certain way; arrange according to a plan or schedule; broadcast or air a program

programme: British spelling of program

pros: n.; plural of pro (a professional, especially in sports; advantages, as opposed to cons)

     prep. or adv.; in favor of

prose: n.; written or oral language, in its ordinary form

psi: n.; the twenty-third letter of the Greek alphabet

sigh: v.; to let out a long breath that expresses sadness or relief or tiredness

     n.; a long breath expressing sadness or relief or other similar emotion

pupal: adj.; from pupa, an insect in its inactive immature form between larva and adult

pupil: n.; a student in school; the dark, round part of the eye

Q

quail: n.; a type of bird
  v.; show fear
quell: v.; put an end to disorder using force; to silence someone; to soothe
an unpleasant feeling

quarts: n.; plural of quart (two pints or one-fourth of a gallon)
quartz: n.; a type of mineral

quay: n.; a dock or wharf
key: n.; small piece of shaped metal that opens a lock; a button on a
typewriter or telephone or computer keyboard
  adj.; very important
  v.; to enter data on a keyboard

queue: n.; a line of people or vehicles; a list of data stored
  v.; to line up
cue: n.; a signal or prompt or reminder
  v.; to give a cue to or for

R

Ra: n.; Ancient Egypt sun god
rah: inter.; a cheer

rabbit: n.; a plant-eating animal with long ears and a short tail
      v.; to hunt rabbits; British slang for talk a long time about something
rabbet: n.; a construction term having to do with joints
      v.; to make a rabbet in a piece of wood

rack: n.; shelf for holding things
      v.; cause extreme pain to; to put in a rack
wrack: v.; alternate spelling of rack

racket: n.; instrument used in some sports; a type of snowshoe; loud noise; an illegal scheme to get money; one's line of work
      v.; to make a loud noise
racquet: n.; alternate spelling of racket; instrument used in sports, especially tennis

Rae: n.; a person's name
ray: n.; a beam (of light or heat)
      v.; spread from a central point
Ray: n.; a last name or a male's first name, as in a nickname for Raymond
re: n.; second note of the musical scale
rey: n.; Spanish for king

raid: n.; a sudden attack
      v.; to conduct a raid on; quickly take something from a place
rayed: v.; past tense of to ray (spread from a central point)

rail: n.; bars that are part of a fence used to hang things on; railroad tracks
v.; provide with a rail; a term in windsurfing; complain strongly about something; a type of bird
rale: n.; a rattling sound in unhealthy lungs

rain: n.; moisture falling from the sky in drops
v.; to come down as rain
reign: v.; to rule or govern
n.; the period a sovereign rules
rein: n.; a strap used to guide a horse
v.; to guide a horse with reins

raise: v.; to lift to a higher position; increase
n.; an increase in salary; an increase in a stake in gambling
rays: n.; plural of ray (a beam of light)
raze: v.; destroy
rase: v.; alternate spelling of raze

raiser: n.; one who raises (lifts up)
razor: n.; instrument with a sharp edge to remove hair from the body
v.; to cut with a razor

rap: v.; strike a surface; talk in an easy, informal manner
n.; a quick knock; type of music of African-American origin
wrap: v.; to cover with a material
n.; a loose outer piece of material like a shawl; the end of filming or recording

rapped: v.; past tense of to rap (see above)
rapt: adj.; fascinated by something
wrapped: v.; past tense of to wrap (cover with a material)

rappel: v.; to go down a surface like a mountain
n.; a descent made by rappelling
repel: v.; to force back; to be disgusting to

rapper: n.; one who raps (see above)
wrapper: n.; something covering something else; a loose robe or gown

read: v; past tense of the verb to read (to look at and understand written material)
red: adj.; of a color next to orange, as of cherries or rubies
    n.; red color; a red thing; owing money or showing a loss

read: v.; to look at and comprehend written material; understand information by reading it in a written source
    n.; one's interpretation of something
reed: n.; a tall plant in the grass family that grows in water
Reed (or Reid): n.; a first or last name

real: adj.; actually existing or not of the imagination; genuine
    adv.; very or really
reel: n.; a cylinder on which some material can be wound; a type of dance
    v.; to wind some material onto a reel; stagger or lose one's balance
rill: n.; a small stream
    v.; to flow like a rill

realize: v.; to become fully aware of something as a fact or to understand it clearly; to cause to happen
realise: British spelling of realize

reata: n.; a long-noosed rope to catch animals
riata: n.; same as above

rebait: v.; to bait again (as on a hook in fishing)
rebate: n.; a partial refund
    v.; pay back a sum of money

recede: v.; to go or move back; gradually diminish
reseed: v.; to seed again (sow an area of land with seed)

receipt: n.; receiving or getting something; a written statement saying that something has been paid for or that goods have been received; amount of money received at a certain time by a business
    v.; to mark a bill as being paid; to write a receipt
reseat: v.; cause someone to sit down again after they have gotten up; to equip with new seats

reckless: adj.; not thinking or caring about an action's consequences
wreckless: adj.; can only mean you haven't had a wreck!

recognize: v.; to identify someone or something you have seen before; to accept something or someone
recognise: v.; British spelling of recognize

reek: v.; smell unpleasantly or stink
    n.; a bad smell
wreak: v.; cause much damage or harm; to inflict vengeance upon

residence: n.; one's home
residents: n.; plural of resident (one who lives in a certain place or a medical graduate practicing under supervision in a hospital)

rest: v.; stop work to relax; be placed so as to stay in a certain position; to lie buried
    n.; a period of time relaxing; in music, an interval of silence
wrest: v.; to take something from one's hands

retch: v.; to vomit or make the sound of vomiting
    n.; movement or sound of vomiting
wretch: n.; unhappy person; a bad person

review: n.; a formal examination of something to make possible changes; an assessment of a play or movie or book
    v.; to assess something to see if changes are needed; to write a review of something
revue: n.; light theatrical entertainment of short sketches like songs and dances

rhea: n.; a South American flightless bird
ria: n.; a long, narrow inlet

rho: n.; the seventeenth letter of the Greek alphabet
roe: n.; fish eggs; a type of deer
row: n.; people or things mostly in a straight line; a line of seats in a theater; a street with a continuous line of houses; a horizontal line of entries in a data table
      v.; to propel a boat with oars

rhyme: n.; sounds that are alike, especially at the ends of lines of poems
      v.; to end with a sound that corresponds to another
rime: n.; a type of frost
      v.; to cover something with frost

ria: n.; a long, narrow water inlet
rhea: n.; a large South American bird that cannot fly

rigger: n.; one who rigs something, especially a ship or aircraft or parachute
rigor: n.; sudden feeling of cold with shivering, fever, and sweating; quality of being very thorough and accurate; strictness and severity; hard conditions

right: adj.; morally good and fair and just; true or correct as a fact
      adv.; completely; correctly
      n.; that which is morally correct and honorable; a moral or legal right to have or get something or to act in a certain way
      v.; to restore to an upright position
rite: n.; a religious or other ceremony or custom or practice
wright: n.; a maker or builder
write: v.; to mark on a surface with a pen, pencil, etc.; to compose and send a letter to someone

ring: n.; a small, round band, usually precious metal, worn on a finger or toe; a circular object
      v.; surround someone or something
wring: v.; twist something to force water from it
      n.; the act of squeezing something

road: n.; a street or highway; series of events leading to a certain outcome
rode: v.; past tense of to ride (to sit on and control the movement of something); be carried by something
rowed: v.; past tense of to row (to propel a boat with oars)

roads: n.; plural of road (see above)
Rhodes: n.; a Greek island

roam: v.; move about with no aim; use a mobile phone on another's network, usually in another country
n.; an aimless walk
Rome: n.; capital and largest city of Italy

roan: adj.; of an animal, having one main-color coat mixed with other colors
n.; an animal with a roan coat
Rhone: n.; a river in Western Europe

roc: n.; a large bird in mythology
rock: n.; solid mineral material; boulder or stone; small piece of cocaine
v.; move gently to and fro or side to side; shake or vibrate; cause great distress to; shock; dance or play rock music

roes: n.; plural of roe (see above)
rose: n.; a type of fragrant flower
rows: n.; plural of row (see above)
v.; part of the verb to row (see above)

roger: inter. (or exclamation); your message has been received and understood
Roger: n; a male name
Rodger: n.; alternate spelling of Roger

role: n.; an actor's part in a movie, etc.; part played by one in a particular situation or position or capacity
roll: v.; turn over and over; move along on wheels
n.; a throw or toss; a cylinder or tube

roo: n.; a kangaroo
roux: n.; a mix of fat and flour to make a sauce
rue: v.; to regret
     n.; a type of shrub

rood: n.; a crucifix; one-fourth of an acre
rude: adj.; impolite or bad-mannered; abrupt or sudden
rued: v.; past tense of to rue (to regret)

roomer: n.; a renter of a room in someone else's home
rumor: n.; a story or report of something that may not be true; gossip
     v.; be circulated as an account of something that may not be true
rumour: n.; British spelling of rumor

root: n.; part of a plant that is usually underground; cause or source of something; the essential nature of something; mathematical term for square root
     v.; to cause a plant to grow roots; establish deeply or embed; have as an origin; to cause to be unable to move from
route: n.; a way taken to get from one place to another
     v.; to send along a specific course

rosy: adj.; like pink or red, as of one's skin tone; hopeful and promising, as of one's future
Rosie: n.; a female name, a nickname for Rose

rote: n.; repetition of something to be learned
wrote: v.; past tense of to write (to mark letters, words, etc., on a surface with a pen, etc.)

rough: adj.; not smooth; not gentle
   adv.; harshly or violently
   n.; a thug or bad person
   v.; shape something in a rough, preliminary way; live in a condition
of having basic necessities only
ruff: n.; a starched frill around the neck; a colored ring of hair or feathers
around the neck of a bird or animal

rouse: v.; awaken; to anger or excite; cause an emotion
rows: n.; plural of row (a noisy quarrel or argument)

rout: n.; retreat or flight of defeated troops
   v.; defeat
route: n.; a way taken to get from one place to another (there are two
pronunciations of this word)

rumor: n.; a current story or report that may not be true
   v.; with -ed, said to be
rumour: n.; British spelling of rumor
roomer: n.; one who rents a room in another's house

rung: n.; horizontal step on a ladder
   v.; past tense of the verb to ring (make a clear sound; chime or toll
or peal)
wrung: v.; past tense of to wring (squeeze something to force liquid out
of it)

rye: n.; type of cereal plant; type of whiskey; type of bread
wry: adj.; using dry, mocking humor; twisted into an expression of disgust
or annoyance, as of the face

S

S: n.; the nineteenth letter of the alphabet
ess: n.; the letter S

saber: n.; a type of sword
sabre: n.; British spelling of saber

sac: n.; bag or pouch
sack: n.; a bag used for carrying or storing things; slang for bed
     v.; to fire someone from a job; tackle the quarterback in football
before he throws the ball; to put in a sack

safe: n.; a locked cabinet for storage of valuables
     adj.; protected from danger
seif: n.; type of sand dune

sail: n.; piece of material on a boat that catches wind and propels it; a trip in
a ship or boat
     v.; travel in a boat that has sails; move quickly and smoothly; to begin a
voyage; to steer a boat or ship
sale: n.; the exchange of something for money; the action of selling
something; a period of time in which a retailer sells goods at lower prices

sailer: n.; a sailing ship or boat
sailor: n.; one who sails

sane: adj.; of sound mind; not mentally ill; reasonable and sensible
seine: n.; fishing net
      v.; to fish with a seine
Seine: n.; a river in France, flowing through Paris to the English Channel

satyr: n.; a lustful, drunken god in mythology
Seder: n.; a Jewish ceremony during early Passover

saver: n.; one who saves (keeps something or someone from danger or one who keeps something for future use)
savor: v.; taste and enjoy food or drink
      n.; a taste or flavor or scent, especially a pleasant one
savour: British spelling of savor

scene: n.; location or site; action in a play, movie, etc.; landscape; an incident or episode; area of certain activity
seen: v.; part of the verb to see (perceive with the eyes)

scent: n.; aroma or smell, especially a pleasant one; trail indicated by the smell of an animal
      v.; to detect the smell of
sent: v.; past tense of the verb to send (to cause to go to a certain place)
cent: n.; one penny; one-hundredth of a dollar

scents: n.; plural of scent (see above)
sense: n.; feeling of sight, smell, hearing, taste, and touch; awareness
      v.; to perceive by a sense or senses
cents: n.; plural of cent (see above)

sceptic: n.; British spelling of skeptic (one that questions an opinion)
skeptic: n.; preferred spelling of sceptic in North America and Canada

scull: n.; one of the two oars used to row a boat
      v.; to propel a boat with sculls
skull: n.; the skeleton of the head of a person or animal

sea: n.; ocean
see: v.; perceive with the eyes; understand
sí: Spanish and Italian for yes

seal: n.; something used to join two things together; a material with a design stamped into it; a fish-eating aquatic mammal
      v.; to fasten or close; apply a waterproof coating
sill: n.; a type of shelf at the bottom of a window
ceil: v.; old-fashioned word meaning to plaster the roof of a building

sealing: v.; part of the verb to seal (fasten securely; apply a coating to a surface)
ceiling: n.; top interior surface of a room; upper limit

seam: n.; the line along which two pieces of fabric are sewn; an underground layer
      v.; to join with a seam
seem: v.; appear to be

seamen: n.; plural of seaman (sailor)
semen: n.; male reproductive fluid

sear: v.; scorch or burn; alternate spelling of sere
seer: n.; one who is possibly able to see the future
sere: adj.; dry and withered; alternate spelling of sear

seas: n.; plural of sea (ocean)
sees: v.; part of the verb to see (perceive with the eyes)
seize: v.; take hold of quickly and forcibly

sects: n.; plural of sect (a group of people with different religious beliefs from those of a larger group to which they belong)
sex: n.; intercourse or love-making; gender (male or female)

seed: n.; a flowering plant's unit of reproduction; a man's semen
    v.; sow with seeds; produce or drop seeds
cede: v.; to give up or yield

seeder: n.; one who seeds (see above)
cedar: n.; type of evergreen tree
ceder: n.; one who cedes (see above)

seek: v.; to go in search of
Sikh: n.; member of a religious sect in India

sell: v.; give something in exchange for money
    n.; act of selling
cell: n.; a small room for a prisoner, especially; smallest structural,
functioning unit of an organism

seller: n.; one who sells (see above)
cellar: n.; room below the ground; basement
    v.; store in a cellar

send: v.; to cause to go from one place to another
sinned: v.; past tense of sin (offend against God or a person)
scend: n.; old-fashioned term for the surge of a wave
    v.; to surge in a stormy sea

serf: n.; laborer or servant or slave
surf: n.; foam formed by waves in the sea

serge: n.; a type of woolen fabric
    v.; to sew a fabric to prevent fraying
surge: n.; a sudden rush or outpouring
    v.; move suddenly forward

serial: n.; a story or play presented in regular installments
  adj.; taking part in a series; committing the same crime over and over
cereal: n.; a grain such as wheat, oats, or corn; breakfast food of roasted grain, eaten with milk usually

series: n.; a number of things coming one after the other; sequence; a set of related television or radio programs
Ceres: n.; goddess of agriculture in mythology

serious: adj.; demanding careful consideration; acting or speaking sincerely and earnestly
Sirius: n.; the brightest star in the sky
cereus: n.; type of cactus

session: n.; meeting; period of a particular activity
cession: n.; the giving up of rights or property

sew: v.; to join or repair by making stitches with a needle and thread
so: adv.; to a great extent
  conj.; for this reason why or therefore; with the intention of or in order that
sow: v.; to plant seed

sewer: n.; one who sews (clothes)
soar: v.; to fly high in the air; increase rapidly
sore: adj.; painful and aching
  n.; a raw and painful place in the body; cause of distress or annoyance
sower: n.; one who sows (to plant seeds)

sewer: n.; underground pipe that carries off drainage water or waste
suer: n.; one who sues (takes legal action against)

sex: n.; male or female; intercourse
sects: n.; plural of sect (group of people who broke from the established church)

shear: v.; cut the wool off of an animal; break off due to a structural problem

n.; a strain in something's structure

sheer: adj.; nothing other than or absolute; perpendicular or nearly perpendicular; thin, as in fabric

adv.; perpendicularly

n.; a very thin fabric

v.; swerve or change course; move away from an unpleasant topic

sheik: n.; an Arab leader, also spelled sheikh

chic: adj.; stylish

n.; stylishness and elegance

shoe: n.; a foot covering

v.; to fit a horse with a shoe

shoo: inter.; a word said to scare a person or animal away

v.; to make a person or animal go away by waving arms, for example

shone: v.; past tense of the verb to shine (to give out light)

shown: v.; part of the verb to show (cause to be visible; display)

shoot: v.; wound or kill a person or animal with a bullet or arrow; move suddenly and quickly in a certain direction

n.; a young branch of a tree; when a group of people hunt and shoot animals

chute: n.; a slope like a slide to send things to a lower level; a narrow enclosure for holding livestock for branding or vaccinating, etc.

shop: n.; place where goods or services are sold; a store

v.; to visit a store to buy something

shoppe: n.; a deliberate spelling of shop to show old-fashioned charm

sic: adv.; used in brackets after words that seem odd or incorrect in its original form

v.; to set a dog or other animal on someone

sick: adj.; having physical or mental illness

side: n.; a position to the left or right; part of a surface that is not the top or bottom or front or back; a particular aspect of a person or situation
      v.; to support or oppose
sighed: v.; past tense of to sigh (let out a long, deep breath that shows sadness or relief or fatigue)

sigh: v.; see above
Sy: n.; a male name
Cy: n.; a male name

sigher: n.; one who sighs (see above)
sire: n.; male parent of an animal, especially a stallion or bull; a respectful form of address to a king, etc.

sighs: n.; plural of sigh (see above)
      v.; part of the verb to sigh
size: n.; the extent or dimensions of something; how big something is; how clothing is divided
      v.; to change the size of something or to sort by size

sight: n.; the sense of sight; something than can be seen
      v.; to see someone or something; take aim on a gun
site: n.; area on which something is constructed; a website
      v.; to build something in a certain place
cite: v.; to quote a passage, book, or author; to praise someone for a brave act; to mention as an example; in law, refer to a prior case; to summon someone to appear in court

sign: n.; an indication or signal of something; a gesture used to give information; short for sign language
      v.; write one's name; use gestures to convey information; use sign language
sine: n.; in mathematics, one of the trigonometric functions
syne: adv.; Scottish for ago

signet: n.; official seal or stamp
cygnet: n.; a young swan

sink: v.; go below the surface, especially of a liquid; become submerged; descend; of a ship, to go to the bottom of a body of water; cause a ship or boat to go to the bottom of a body of water; cause to fail; to fall or drop
n.; a basin with a water supply and drain
sync: n.; synchronization
v.; to synchronize (occur at the same time or rate)

sir: n.; used as a respectful way to address a man
sur: n.; Spanish for south

ski: n.; each of a pair of long, narrow pieces of a hard, flexible material attached to the feet for gliding on snow
v.; to travel over snow on skis
skee: n.; alternate spelling of ski; part of an arcade game called Skee-Ball

slay: v.; to kill a person or animal; to amuse someone greatly
sleigh: n.; a sled
v.; ride on a sleigh

sleight: n.; use of skill to deceive someone
slight: adj.; small or little; of a person, not strongly built
v.; insult someone by being disrespectful or inattentive
n.; an insult caused by disrespect or inattention

slew: n.; a large group of things
v.; slide or skid; past tense of to slay (see above)
slough: n.; a swamp; situation of no progress or activity
slue: alternate spelling of slew

sloe: n.; fruit of the blackthorn
slow: adj.; not fast; of a clock, showing a time earlier than what is correct; not quick to comprehend
adv.; at a slow pace or slowly
v.; reduce speed

soared: v.; past tense of soar (see above)
sword: n.; a type of weapon with a long blade

soccer: n.; type of sport with a ball that cannot be touched with hands or arms
socker: n.; one who socks (hits forcefully)

socks: n.; plural of sock (a garment for the foot; a hard hit)
      v.; part of the verb to sock (to hit with force)
sox: n.; nonstandard plural spelling of sock (foot covering)

solar: adj.; having to do with the sun
soler: n.; one who soles shoes

sold: v.; past tense of the verb to sell (see above)
      adj.; excited about something
soled: v.; past tense of to sole (put a new sole on, as on a shoe)

sol: n.; the fifth note of a major scale
sole: n.; the undersurface of one's foot or shoe; a type of fish
      v.; put a new sole on a shoe
      adj.; the one and only
soul: n.; the spiritual part of a human being or animal; feeling or emotion; the essence of something; an individual person; African-American pride
Seoul: n.; capital of South Korea

somber: adj.; rather gloomy or solemn
sombre: adj.; British spelling of somber

some: adj.; a number of
      pron.; an unspecified number of people or things
      adv.; to some extent or somewhat
sum: n.; an amount of money; total in addition
      v.; to find the sum

son: n.; a male child
sun: n.; the star around which Earth orbits; warmth from the sun
      v.; to lie or sit in the sun

sonny: n.; used by an older person to address a young boy
sunny: adj.; bright with sunlight; with respect to a person, cheerful

sou: n.; small amount of money; an old French coin
Sioux: n.; the Native American Dakota people or their language
       adj.; relating to the Sioux
sue: v.; bring legal proceedings against
Sue: n.; a female name, short for Susan or Suzanne
sous: French for subordinate as in sous-chef

spade: n.; tool for digging and cutting ground
       v.; dig in the ground with a spade
spayed: v.; past tense of to spay (sterilize a female animal by removing her ovaries)

spear: n.; a long weapon with a pointed tip; an instrument used to catch fish
       v.; to strike with a spear
speer: v.; to ask
speir: v.; alternate spelling of speer

specialize: v.; concentrate on and become an expert in a certain skill or subject
specialise: v.; British spelling of specialize

specter: n.; a ghost or any possible dangerous occurrence
spectre: n.; British spelling of specter

spits: v.; part of the verb to spit (eject saliva from the mouth)
       n.; plural of spit (a long, thin skewer for meat when roasting)
spitz: n.; type of dog breed

staff: n.; the people employed by a business; officers assisting a commanding officer in the military; a long stick to aid in walking; a scepter; in music, the five lines and the spaces between them

v.; to provide with a staff

staph: n.; short for staphylococcus, a type of bacteria

staid: adj.; quiet and serious

stayed: v.; past tense of to stay (remain in the same place)

stair: n.; a set of steps or a single step in a set of stairs

stare: v.; look at someone or something with eyes wide open

n.; a long fixed look

stere: n.; a unit of volume equal to one cubic meter

stake: n.; a wooden or metal post with a point on one end to support something

v.; to support with a stake; mark an area with stakes to claim ownership of it

steak: n.; thick slice of beef or other meat or fish

stanch: v.; stop blood flowing from a wound

staunch: adj.; a newer form of stanch; of a wall of strong or firm construction

standardization: n.; process of making something conform to a standard (a level of quality)

standardisation: n.; British spelling of standardization

stationary: adj.; not moving or changing

stationery: n.; writing paper, especially with matching envelopes

steal: v.; take another one's property; thieve; sneak somewhere quietly
      n.; a bargain, as at a store; act of stealing something
steel: n.; hard, strong alloy of iron used in building
      v.; mentally prepare to do or face something difficult
still: adj.; not moving and very quiet
      n.; silence and calm; a single shot from a movie
      adv.; up to this time; nevertheless or all the same
      v.; to make or become still; to quieten

stent: n.; a tube put inside a blood vessel, for example, to relieve an obstruction; a tax
      v.; to tax
stint: n.; one's fixed period of work; a type of bird
      v.; supply an amount of something that is not enough

step: n.; putting one leg in front of the other while walking or running; a stair
      v.; to walk
steppe: n.; large area of grassland in southeastern Europe or Siberia

sticks: n.; plural of stick (piece of wood or a long, thin piece of something)
      v.; part of the verb to stick (push a pointy object into something)
Styx: n.; a river in the underworld in mythology

stile: n.; an arrangement of steps allowing people to climb over a fence or wall;
style: n.; the manner of doing something; distinctive appearance
      v.; design or make in a certain way

stint: n.; one's fixed period of work; a type of bird
      v.; supply an inadequate amount of something
stent: n.; in medicine, a tube put in the body to help the body heal or relieve a blockage; a property assessment; a tax
      v.; to charge for purposes of taxing

stoep: n.; a porch in front of a house in South Africa

stoop: v.; to bend one's head or body over downward; lower one's moral standards

n.; posture in which the head and shoulders are bent forward; the downward swoop of a bird of prey

stoup: n.; a basin for holy water

story: n.; a tale of people and events for entertainment; account of events in one's life; part of a building made up of rooms on the same floor

storey: n.; British spelling of story

straight: adj.; in one direction only and uncurving; properly aligned; honest; in order; of alcohol, undiluted; hetrosexual; not under the influence of drugs

adv.; in a straight line; directly

n.; part of something not curved, as on a racetrack; in poker, a continuous sequence of five cards

strait: n.; a narrow body of water connecting two other larger bodies of water

sty: n.; a pigpen; an infection on the eyelid

v.; to keep a pig in a sty

stye: n.; alternate spelling of sty of the eye

succor: n.; aid or help

v.; to give assistance to

sucker: n.; an easily deceived person; a type of candy; something that sucks (clings to the surface)

v.; to trick someone

succour: British spelling of succor

suede: n.; a type of velvety leather

swayed: v.; past tense of the verb to sway (move slowly back and forth or side to side; control or influence someone or something)

suite: n.; a set of rooms; set of instrumental compositions or pieces from an opera
sweet: adj.; tasting of sugar; pleasing and delightful
       n.; something with sugar in it

sundae: n.; ice cream with other added ingredients
Sunday: n.; the first day of the week before Monday and part of the weekend
       adv.; on Sunday

swell: v.; become larger in size, especially on the body
       n.; gently rounded shape; gradual increase in sound or amount
       adj.; slang for excellent
       adv.; slang for very well or excellently
swale: n.; low place, like a ditch or trench

symbol: n.; something that stands for something else; a character or mark or letter
cymbal: n.; musical instrument that is concave, round, and brass that makes a ringing or clashing sound when struck with a stick, as in a drum set, or by another cymbal

symbolize: v.; be a symbol (something that stands for something else) of
symbolise: British spelling of symbolize

T

tach: n.; short for tachometer (instrument for measuring the speed of an engine)
tack: n.; small type of nail with a broad head; a long stitch used to fasten fabrics together temporarily
     v.; to fasten with tacks; in sailing, to change course by turning into the wind

tacked: v.; past tense of to tack (see above)
tact: n.; sensitivity and understanding when dealing with others

tacks: n.; plural of tack (see above)
tax: n.; contribution to state or federal revenue; burden or heavy demand
     v.; impose a tax on; make heavy demands on someone

tail: n.; back end of an animal; something that looks like a tail
     v.; follow someone closely and secretly
tale: n.; a story
tell: v.; communicate information; decide correctly about something
     n.; an action that betrays an attempted deception

tailer: v.; one who tails (see above); a type of fish
tailor: n.; one who makes clothes
     v.; to make clothes to fit an individual
Taylor: n.; a first or last name

taper: v.; to become thinner toward one end
     n.; a thin candle; gradual narrowing
tapir: n.; a type of nocturnal, hoofed mammal

tare: n.; a type of weed; a type of plant in the pea family
tear: v.; to rip apart; move quickly rather carelessly
     n.; a hole in something after being ripped apart; brief time of unrestrained behavior or binge or spree

taught: v.; past tense of to teach (educate or instruct)
taut: adj.; tight, not slack; tense; concise

tea: n.; drink made with leaves of the tea plant; the shrub that produces tea leaves
tee: n.; space on a golf course where the ball is hit at the beginning of each hole; the peg that supports a golf ball before it is hit; in football, a stand on which the ball is placed before it is kicked; stand used in tee-ball; a T-shirt; the letter T
     v.; to place a ball on a tee; move a ball into position, as in soccer
ti: n.; the seventh note of a major scale

team: n.; a group of players on one side in a game or sport
     v.; come together as a team to accomplish a goal; match a piece of clothing with another
teem: v.; to be full of or alive with or overflowing with; pour down or fall heavily, as rain

tear: n.; drop of clear liquid that comes from the eye when crying, for example
     v.; produce tears
tier: n.; a row or level of a structure

teas: n.; plural of tea (see above)
tease: v.; make fun of in a playful way; pull strands of hair separately
     n.; one who makes fun of someone; one who flirts with someone else with no other intentions
tees: n.; plural of tee (see above)

teepee: n.; a tent that looks like a cone, used by Native Americans
tipi: n.; alternate spelling of teepee

tense: adj.; stretched tight, like a muscle
   v.; to become tense, especially from nervousness
   n.; one of the forms of a verb
tents: n.; plural of tent (a temporary shelter made of cloth)

tent: n.; see above
tint: n.; a shade of a color; a dye for coloring the hair
   v.; to color something

tern: n.; a seabird related to the gull
turn: v.; move in a circular direction; put in a different position
   n.; the act of turning; a change of direction when moving

testee: n.; one who takes an examination
testy: adj.; bad-tempered or grumpy

the: adj.; denoting one or more people or things already mentioned
thee: pron.; old form of you

theater: n.; a place where plays and other types of drama are performed
theatre: n.; British spelling of theater

their: pron.; a possessive pronoun used in front of a noun; of people or
things already mentioned
there: adv.; in, at, or to that place
they're: contraction for they are

threw: v.; past tense of to throw (propel something)
through: prep.; moving in one side and out the other
    adv.; continuing to completion of something
    adj.; direct
thru: nonstandard spelling of through

throes: n.; pain and struggle
throws: v.; part of the verb to throw (to propel something through the air with the arm and hand; cause to suddenly enter into a certain condition)
        n.; acts of throwing; plural of throw (a covering for furniture)

throne: n.; a royal chair
thrown: v.; part of the verb to throw (see throw)

throw: v.; propel something with force through the air with the arm and hand; cause to enter a certain condition suddenly
        n.; act of covering something; a light cover for furniture
throe: n.; severe pain or struggle

thyme: n.; an herb in the mint family
time: n.; past, present, and future; a point of time or hour of the day
        v.; plan when something should happen; measure the time taken to do something

tic: n.; a spasm of a muscle, usually in the face; strange habit of one's behavior
tick: n.; a short, sharp sound, especially by a clock or watch; a check mark; a parasitic insect in the spider family that sucks blood
        v.; make a ticking sound; to make a check mark

tide: n.; the rising and falling of the sea
tied: v.; past tense of the verb to tie (attach with string or cord; restrict to a certain thing or place); connected or linked
        adj.; in sports, when both teams have the same score

tier: n.; one who ties (fastens something or someone with string or cord)
tire: v.; feel the need for rest; to become bored with
        n.; rubber covering around a wheel on a vehicle
tyre: n.; British spelling of tire; outdated form of tier

'til: prep. or conj.; short for until (up to the point in time or event mentioned)

till: prep. or conj.; another informal way to say until (see above)
      n.; a cash register drawer to hold money
      v.; to prepare land for crops

teal: n.; a dark greenish-blue color; a type of duck

timber: n.; wood for building; lumber
          inter.; used to warn that a tree is about to fall

timbre: n.; quality of a musical sound; tone

to: prep.; expressing motion in the direction of; approaching or reaching
    adv.; so as to be closed or almost closed
    v.; used with the base form of a verb to show the infinitive form

too: adv.; more than enough; also

two: n.; the number 2

toad: n.; type of amphibian, similar to a frog; a bad person

toed: v.; past tense of to toe (push or touch something with one's toe)
      adj.; having toes

towed: v.; past tense of to tow (pull a vehicle with a chain or rope or other towing manner)

toe: n.; one of the five digits on the human foot; the end or tip of something
    v.; push or touch something with one's toe

tow: v. pull a vehicle with a chain or rope
    n.; the act of towing

told: v.; past tense of to tell (communicate information; decide correctly)

tolled: v.; past tense of to toll (charge a fee for using a particular bridge or road; of a bell, rang out)

ton: n.; 2000 pounds, or a little over 900 kg, in the United States and Canada

tonne: n.; a metric system measure, 1000 kg

tool: n.; instrument, usually handheld, used for a particular task
v.; to put a design on, especially a book; to equip with tools
tulle: n.; type of soft material like net used for veils and dresses

toon: n.; short for cartoon
tune: n.; a melody, especially of a certain piece of music
v.; adjust a musical instrument to the correct pitch

tooter: n.; one who toots (sounds a horn or other device with a short, sharp sound; one who snorts cocaine)
tutor: n.; a private teacher
v.; act as a tutor to one student or a very small group of children
Tudor: adj.; relating to the British royal dynasty who held the throne from 1485-1603
n.; a member of the Tudor dynasty

tor: n.; a hill or rocky peak
tore: v.; past tense of tear (to rip apart; move very fast and excitedly)

tour: n.; a pleasure trip; journey made by performers or sports teams to perform or play
v.; take a tour of an area
Tours: n.; city in West France on the Loire River

tracked: v.; past tense of the verb to track (follow the trail or course of someone or something to find them or keep an eye on them)
tract: n.; an area of land, usually large; a major passage in the body

transience: n.; the state of lasting only a short time
transients: n.; plural of transient (one who works or stays in a place for just a short time)

traumatize: v.; to cause to go into shock due to a disturbing experience or injury
traumatise: v.; British spelling of traumatize

traveled: v.; past tense of to travel (to take a trip or to move in a constant way)
travelled: v.; British spelling of traveled

traveler: n.; one who is traveling or often travels (see above)
traveller: n.; British spelling of traveler

tray: n.; a flat, shallow container used for carrying food or drink
trey: n.; in basketball, a shot worth three points; a playing card or die with three spots

troop: n.; soldiers
      v.; come or go in large numbers
troupe: n.; group of entertainers who tour to different places

trooper: n.; a state police officer; soldier
trouper: n.; an entertainer, especially one with much experience; a reliable, uncomplaining person

trussed: v.; past tense of to truss (tie the wings and legs of poultry before cooking; support with a truss, a type of support for a bridge, etc.)
trust: n.; belief or faith in someone or something; an arrangement where one holds property for the good of someone else; a monopoly
      v.; have faith or confidence in; put in the hands of or entrust one with something

trustee: n.; agent
trusty: n.; a prisoner who is given special privileges and responsibilities for good behavior
      adj.; having served for a long time and seen as reliable and faithful

U

urn: n.; a large vase, especially one used for keeping the ashes of a cremated person; a metal container with a tap, used for making coffee or tea or for boiling water
earn: v.; to get money in return for a service or labor
erne: n.; type of sea eagle

use: v.; take or hold something in order to achieve a result; employ; consume an amount from a limited supply
ewes: n.; plural of ewe (female sheep)
yews: n.; plural of yew, a type of cone-bearing poisonous tree with red berries

V

V: n.; the twenty-second letter of the English alphabet
vee: n.; the letter V or something shaped like a V; Roman numeral for 5

vain: adj.; having a high opinion of one's self; conceited; producing no result
vane: n.; part of a windmill or propeller; short for weathervane; also part of a feather
vein: n.; tube that carries blood to the heart; rock fracture containing minerals or ore; streak of a different color in something; specific quality or style

vale: n.; valley
veil: n.; piece of material worn by a woman to conceal the face
      v.; cover with a veil

valor: n.; great courage in the face of danger
valour: n.; British spelling of valor

venous: adj.; relating to veins
Venus: n.; Roman goddess of beauty and love; second planet from the sun

vial: n.; a small container, especially used for liquid medicine
vile: adj.; very unpleasant or wicked
viol: n.; type of stringed musical instrument

vigor: n.; good health and physical strength; effort and enthusiasm
vigour: n.; British spelling of vigor

visualize: v.; to imagine or form a mental image
visualise: v.; British spelling of visualize

W

wax: n.; substance secreted by bees; earwax
      v.; cover with wax; remove unwanted hair from the body; become larger, as the moon; become stronger
WACS: n.; the women from the Women's Army Corps during WWII
whacks: n.; plural of whack (a hard hit; an attempt or try)
          v.; part of the verb to whack (strike hard with a blow)

waddle: v.; walk with short steps in a clumsy, swaying motion
          n.; a waddling type of walk
wattle: n.; fence material made of stakes mixed with twigs and branches; the colored flesh hanging from the head or neck of fowl
      v.; to make with wattle

wade: v.; walk through water
      n.; an act of wading
weighed: v.; past tense of to weigh (find out how heavy someone or something is; assess the importance of or the consequences of)

wail: n.; a long, high-pitched cry of pain or grief or anger
      v.; to give a cry of pain or grief or anger
wale: n.; a ridge on material like corduroy; plank running alongside a ship to protect its hull
whale: n.; large sea mammal; leviathan
      v.; beat or hit

wailer: n.; one who wails (see above)
whaler: n.; whaling ship or a seaman in the act of whaling

wails: v.; part of the verb to wail (see above)
Wales: n.; part of the United Kingdom in southwest Great Britain

wain: n.; a wagon
wane: v.; to become smaller
Wayne: n.; a male name

waist: n.; part of the body below the ribs and above the hips
waste: v.; to use carelessly or squander; become weaker
      adj.; of a substance thrown away; of an area of land not used
      n.; the act of using something carelessly; material not wanted

wait: v.; stay where one is or stand by; used to show that one is eager to do something or for something to happen
      n.; a period of waiting
weight: n.; the heaviness of someone or something; a piece of metal of a certain weight used to see how heavy something is
      v.; hold something down by placing something heavy on it; attach importance to

waive: v.; refuse to insist on or use a right; refrain from enforcing a rule or fee
wave: v.; move one's hand to and fro as a greeting or signal; move to and fro or sway, like a flag
      n.; long body of water curled and breaking on a shore; sudden occurrence or increase in something
WAVE: n.; female member of the women's branch of the U. S. Naval Reserve during World War II (Women Accepted for Voluntary Emergency)

waiver: n.; an act of waiving a right or claim; document recording the waiving of a right or claim
waver: n.; one who waves (see above)
      v.; to become unsteady or stagger; to be undecided about something

walk: v.; move at a regular pace by lifting and setting down each foot in turn; accompany or escort
      n.; act of traveling on foot; route marked out for walking
wok: n.; bowl-shaped frying pan used in Chinese cooking

wan: adj.; pale or white in complexion
Juan: n.; a male name, Spanish for John

want: v.; have a desire to possess or do something; should or need to do something

       n.; lack of something; desire for something

wont: n.; custom or habit

       adj.; of a person in the habit of doing something

won't: contraction for will not

war: n.; armed conflict or combat

       v.; participate in a war

wore: v.; past tense of to wear (be clothed in; damage or erode or destroy)

ward: n.; part of a hospital for a certain kind of patient; district of a city

       v.; protect or guard; admit a patient to a hospital ward

warred: v.; past tense of the verb to war (see above)

ware: n.; pottery; articles made of a certain type; articles for sale

wear: v.; have on one's body as clothing, etc.; damage by friction

       n.; the wearing of something; clothing for a specific purpose

where: adv.; in or to what place

       conj.; that; whereas

warn: v.; inform one of danger or other unpleasant situation

worn: v.; part of the verb to wear (see above)

       adj.; damaged and shabby from much use

watt: n.; unit of power

what: pron.; asking for information; the thing that, used when specifying something

       adj.; asking for information specifying something; whatever

       adv.; to what extent

wax: n.; sticky substance from honeybees

       v.; to cover with wax

whacks: n.; plural of whack (a sharp hit)

way: n.; course of action or process; road for traveling on

weigh: v.; find out how heavy someone or something is; to think about something in order to make a decision

whey: n.; a watery part of milk, especially in cheese-making

we: pron.; used by one to refer to himself or herself and one or more people together
wee: adj.; small in size or extent
whee: inter.; used to express delight or excitement

weak: adj.; lacking physical strength or energy; lacking power; not able to fulfill its functions properly; of a low standard; unconvincing; easily damaged
week: n.; 7 days, beginning on Sunday and ending on Saturday

weakened: adj.; in a fragile state
              v.; part of the verb to weaken (make or become weaker in power or strength)
weekend: n.; period of time from Friday evening to Sunday evening

weather: n.; climate conditions
              v.; wear away or erode; come safely through a storm
whether: conj.; expressing a doubt or choice between alternatives

weave: v.; form fabric by interlacing thread
              n.; certain way something is woven; type of hairstyle
we've: contraction for we have

we'd: contraction for we had
weed: n.; an unwanted, wild plant
              v.; remove unwanted plants

weld: v.; join together with heating and melting
              n.; a welded joint
welled: v.; past tense of the verb to well (of a liquid, rise to surface and spill or be about to spill; of an emotion, become more intense)

welp: inter.; slang for well
whelp: n.; a puppy
              v.; to give birth to a puppy

wend: v.; go slowly and indirectly in a certain direction
wind: n.; movement of air; breeze; breath needed for physical activity

were: v.; past tense of the verb to be (exist)
whir: v.; make a low, continuous sound, especially of a machine
        n.; a low, continuous regular sound

we're: contraction of we are
weir: n.; a low dam built across a river to raise the water level or regulate its flow; an enclosed set of stakes in a stream for trapping fish

wet: adj.; not dry or, informally, weak
       v.; cover with liquid
       n.; liquid that makes something wet
whet: v.; to sharpen a blade or one's appetite for food

wheel: n.; a round object that revolves on an axle
         v.; to push or pull or carry; to turn around quickly
will: v.; denoting future tense of events
       n.; determination; a legal document containing instructions about what is to be done with one's property after death
we'll: contraction of we will or we shall
weal: n.; a red, swollen mark left on the skin by pressure or a blow
wheal: n.; alternate spelling of weal

when: adv.; at what time; at or on which
        conj.; at or during the time that; after which; and just then
win: v.; to be successful in a contest or conflict
      n.; victory or triumph

which: pron.; asking for information about people or things from a certain set; used referring to something previously mentioned
witch: n.; woman thought to have magic powers, especially evil ones; ugly, unpleasant woman
        v.; cast an evil spell on

while: n.; period of time; at the same time; meanwhile
       conj.; during the time that; at the same time as; whereas
       adv.; during which
       v.; pass time leisurely
wile: n.; trick or scheme
      v.; to lure or entice

whirled: v.; past tense of the verb to whirl (move round and round quickly)
world: n.; the earth; a region or group of countries

whither: adv.; to what place or state; to which
wither: v.; to become dry and shriveled, as a plant; fall into decay or decline

whoa: inter.; used to express surprise or alarm; used to make a horse or human stop or slow down or wait
woe: n.; great sorrow; misery; troubles

whole: adj.; all of; entire; in an unbroken state; in one piece
　　　　n.; something complete in itself; all of something
　　　　adv.; used to emphasize the newness of something
hole: n.; a hollow place in a solid surface
　　　　v.; to make a hole; hit a golf ball so that it falls in a hole

wholly: adv.; entirely or fully
holy: adj.; sacred
holey: adj.; full of holes

who's: contraction for who is or who has
whose: pron.; belonging to or associated with which person; of whom or which

wig: n.; covering of the head made with real or artificial hair
Whig: n.; a member of a British political party; an American colonist who supported the American Revolution

wild: adj.; living and growing in the natural environment, as of a plant or animal; uninhabited place
Wilde: n.; a last name
wiled: v.; past tense of to wile (lure or entice)

wind: v.; take a twisting course; enfold someone or something; turn something round and round, like a clock
wined: v.; past tense of to wine (entertain one by giving them drinks and a meal)

wine: n.; an alcoholic drink made with grape juice
whine: v.; give a long, high-pitched complaining cry
       n.; a long, high-pitched complaining cry; a whimper

won: v.; past tense of to win (be successful in a contest or conflict; get something in a contest or conflict)
one: the number 1
      pron.; referring to a person or thing previously mentioned; one of a specified kind

wood: n.; hard material on the trunk of a tree; area of land covered with trees
would: v.; past tense of the verb will (expressing events that are to be; future tense) indicating the consequence of an imagined event or situation

worst: adv.; most severely or seriously
      n.; the most serious or unpleasant thing that could happen
      v.; get the better of or defeat
wurst: n.; German or Austrian sausage

wrack: v.; alternate spelling of rack; a type of seaweed
rack: v.; cause much physical or mental pain to

wrap: v.; cover or enclose someone or something in paper or other material
      n.; loose outer piece of clothing; end of a session of filming or recording
rap: v.; strike a hard surface with quick blows to attract attention; talk or chat in an easy manner; criticize sharply; to rap to music
      n.; a quick, sharp knock or blow; type of popular music of Black origin; a criminal charge; one's reputation, usually bad

wreak: v.; cause much damage or harm
reek: v.; smell bad or stink
     n.; a bad smell

wrest: v.; forcibly pull something from someone's grasp
rest: v.; stop work and relax; place so as to stay in a certain position
     n.; a period of relaxing; in music, a period of silence

wretch: n.; unhappy person; a bad person
retch: v.; vomit
     n.; a movement or sound of vomiting

wring: v.; squeeze to force liquid from
     n.; act of squeezing or twisting something
ring: n.; small, circular band, usually a precious metal worn on a finger or toe; any ring-shaped object; people arranged in a circle; roped enclosure for sports; act of causing a bell to sound or the sound caused by this; each of a series of vibrating sounds from a telephone; a telephone call; a loud clear tone; a certain quality conveyed by something else
     v.; surround for protection or containment; form a line around the edge of something circular; draw a circle around something; make a clear sound like a shot or bell or alarm; be filled with buzzing or humming as in one's ear; to be filled with; convey a certain impression

write: v.; mark letters, etc., on a surface with a pen, pencil. etc.; compose and send a letter
wright: n.; a maker or builder
right: adj.; good and honest; true or correct
     adv.; completely or totally
     n.; that which is morally correct; legal entitlement
     v.; to put in an upright position
     inter.; used to show one's agreement
rite: n.; religious or other solemn ceremony

wrote: v.; past tense of to write (see above)
rote: n.; repetition of something to be learned

wrung: v.; past tense of the verb to wring (see above)
rung: v.; past tense of the verb to ring (see above)

wry: adj.; using mocking humor; sarcastic; with a look of disgust or annoyance
rye: n.; a cereal plant; whiskey with fermented rye; type of bread

X

X: n.; the twenty-fourth letter of the English alphabet; unknown person or thing; a symbol that looks like an x; Roman numeral for 10; a movie rating, meaning for adults only; short for the drug ecstasy

    v.; mark or make a sign with an x

ex: n.; former husband or wife or partner; the letter X

Y

Y: n.; the twenty-fifth letter of the English alphabet; short for YMCA/ YWCA
why: adv.; for what reason or cause
    conj.; for example, "why you did it"

Yale: n.; a type of lock; a university in New Haven, Connecticut
yell: v.; give a loud cry
    n.; a loud cry, especially of pain or happiness

y'all: contraction for you all
yawl: n.; a type of sailboat

yen: n.; the basic monetary unit of Japan
yin: n.; in Chinese philosophy, the female principle associated with earth, dark, and cold

yep: inter.; nonstandard exclamation meaning yes
yelp: n.; a short, sharp cry of pain or alarm
    v.; to make such a sound
Yelp: n.; a company that reviews businesses

yew: n.; type of tree
you: pron.; used to refer to a person or people that the speaker is addressing; used to refer to anyone in general
ewe: n.; a female sheep

yoke: n.; a wooden crosspiece over the necks of two animals attached to a plow or cart; part of a piece of clothing
yolk: n.; yellow part of an egg

you'll: contraction for you will or you shall
Yule: n.; Christmas

your: pron.; belonging to the person or people the speaker is addressing; belonging to or associated with anyone in general
you're: contraction for you are

Z

Z: n.; the twenty-sixth letter of the English alphabet
zee: n.; the letter Z

Zen: n.; a Japanese school of Buddhism
zin: n.; short for zinfandel, a type of black-skinned wine

Bibliography

Magic Keys, 2020, www.MagicKeys.com/

Merriam-Webster's Collegiate Dictionary, Eleventh Edition. Springfield, MA: Merriam-Webster Incorporated. 2003.

Merriam-Webster, 2020, www.merriam-webster.com/

Newhouse, Dora. Homonyms/Homonimos. Los Angeles, CA: Newhouse Press. 1978.

Singularis, 2020, www.singularis.ltd.uk/

Your Dictionary, 2020, www.YourDictionary.com/

www.ingramcontent.com/pod-product-compliance
Lightning Source LLC
Chambersburg PA
CBHW022010080426
42733CB00007B/550